GO BIG

with Small Groups

Eleven Steps to an Explosive Small Group Ministry

D1024232

BILL EASUM
JOHN ATKINSON

ABINGDON PRESS / Nashville

GO BIG WITH SMALL GROUPS
ELEVEN STEPS TO AN EXPLOSIVE SMALL GROUP MINISTRY
Copyright © 2007 by Abingdon Press

This book is printed on acid-free paper.

Library of Congress Cataloging-in-Publication Data

Easum, William M., 1939-
   Go big with small groups : eleven steps to an explosive small group ministry / Bill Easum and John Atkinson.
      p. cm.
   ISBN-13: 978-0-687-49135-3 (pbk. : alk. paper)
   ISBN-10: 0-687-49135-5
   1. Church group work. 2. Small groups. I. Atkinson, John. II. Title.

   BV652.E33 2007
   253'.7—dc22

2006029006

07 08 09 10 11 12 13 14 15 16—10 9 8 7 6 5 4 3 2 1
MANUFACTURED IN THE UNITED STATES OF AMERICA

GO BIG

WITH SMALL GROUPS

More praise for *Go BIG with Small Groups*:

"The transformational power of authentic community is amazing. We are witnessing small groups across America grow lukewarm church members into fully devoted Christ followers who then invite others along for the journey. If you are looking at this book you've already decided small group ministry is an essential part of your church. But how do you get started? How can you build a healthy small group ministry that is led with excellence at every level?

In their book *Go BIG with Small Groups*, Bill Easum and John Atkinson deliver practical tools to start, build, and manage a life-changing small group ministry. If you are ready to start small groups or improve your current program, you will find this book essential to ensure the success of your ministry."
—Steve Eckharft, pastor of membership & small groups, Fellowship of The Woodlands

"Great insights and practical suggestions for the growing church who has a crowd but needs more community. John Atkinson and Bill Easum have laid out a step-by-step, field-tested plan for churches that want to intentionally connect and grow their people in small groups."
—Dan Lentz, Director, SmallGroups.com

CONTENTS

INTRODUCTION

This book is for leaders who want to know the nuts and bolts of starting or growing a life-changing small group ministry from the ground floor.

Most churches that begin small groups find that within a couple of years two things happen to their small groups: the number of small groups has dwindled in size, and few if any of them have birthed other small groups. So, the only way most churches keep small groups going is by reinventing them over and over, usually with the same people. We know God has much more in store for these churches.

The Greatest Small Group Myth

When we talk with people about small groups we hear the same response: "Our people don't want to split up. They like each other and want to stay together."

Effective small groups seldom split. Most of them multiply when the small group leader and one or two people in the group leave to begin another group. Groups seldom split.

So the secret to small groups that multiply is how well you help the small group leader understand that the goal of small groups is not Bible study or even the small group itself. The goal of small groups is leadership development and multiplication. Small group leaders are effective only if their small group raises up future leaders and multiplies.

This means that all it takes for a small group to multiply is a leader who is capable of raising up his or her replacement and then moving on to begin a new small group.

The Authors

What follows is the wisdom of two practitioners with small groups. John Atkinson is the small group pastor of Bay Area Fellowship in Corpus Christi, Texas, with more than eighteen hundred people in small groups after only four years. Bill Easum was a pastor of one of the largest United Methodist churches in South Texas with more than 70 percent of the people in small groups. Since becoming a consultant, Bill has helped hundreds of churches develop small group ministries.

These are their stories.

John's Story

I woke up one day and found myself called by God to the ministry, though I had no formal training or experience. God called me to one of the fastest-growing churches in America to build and grow a small group ministry. I had led my own group and had served in a volunteer role as the singles small group coordinator, but that was the extent of my knowledge of small groups. On top of that there wasn't anyone at our church with much more experience than I had.

> *This book contains my three-year journey. I hope you can gain some knowledge from my successes and my failures so you don't have to make them too.*
>
> *—John*

The church to which I was called is Bay Area Fellowship in Corpus Christi, Texas. The church was started with five people in the living room of Senior Pastor Bil Cornelius's one-bedroom apartment. Seven and a half years later (2005) the church is doing seven services a weekend with a weekly attendance of around four thousand people.

I began to grow a small group system that would keep up with the rapid growth our church was experiencing. We had about ten groups when I began to serve as a volunteer coordinator and about seventeen when I came on staff. Unfortunately, by the time I came on board the staff, five groups had failed. Two years later we had one hundred seventy groups (2005).

Without anyone to turn to for help, I read every book I could find, attended every conference I could go to, and walked away with a great vision of why God wants us to have small groups in our church. What I didn't walk away with was how to do it. What I wanted to know was, Where do I start from day one? What do I do if the ministry is not growing? Where do I find leaders, how do I train them, how do I get people to join the groups once we have them, and how do I manage them when they're full? I needed practical answers to practical questions, and I couldn't find them.

So I began a journey that was filled with mistakes, failures, and some amazing successes. I was forced to learn a lot in a short period of time because our church was growing so fast that failure wasn't an option. At our current growth rate we would be a big, impersonal church in no time if we didn't connect people relationally along the way.

My hope is you will learn some important lessons from my mistakes so you don't have to make them too. This book is not the end-all to small group ministry. I learn something new every day. But if you have a stagnant ministry or don't have a small group ministry at all, this book can be a guide on your journey to starting or growing a healthy, sustainable, growing small group ministry.

I would love to hear from you if this book has helped you get a small group ministry up and running in your church. E-mail me with your stories, questions, and even criticisms. I hope through your stories, I will be able to learn also from you.

John Atkinson
Hometeams/Discipleship Pastor
Bay Area Fellowship
Corpus Christi, Texas
jccatkinson@aol.com
www.pastorjohnatkinson.com

Bill's Story

I began my experience with small groups in the mid-1980s. My church was not the typical mainline church, but it had many of the trappings of a mainline church. Our small groups were growing and thriving, but then they hit the wall. Because we had so many people on committees and boards it was getting hard to find small group leaders. One day, after someone declined my invitation to be a small group leader, I asked, "If you weren't chair of that committee, would you lead a small group?" She jumped at the chance.

Her response led us to begin telling people that they didn't have to serve on committees if they wanted to lead a small group. In time it became hard to find people who wanted to waste their time in committee work. Then an opportunity arose whereby we were able to drop all of the committees and go to one basic team. Our growth exploded, as did our small groups.

If you are a mainline pastor, don't let your denominational system keep you from jumping into the small groups we write about. Just do it and see what happens. You may be surprised.

Bill Easum
Easum, Bandy & Associates
www.easumbandy.com

Finding Start-up Resources

One of the problems both of us faced when trying to build a small group ministry was that we couldn't find any books that taught us anything about what exactly we were supposed to teach our leaders. All the books taught us a lot about why a church needs a small group ministry, and what it will look like someday when there are thousands of small groups; but we already knew all of that (and you may also). What we couldn't find was a book that would walk us through some kind of a process step by step.

So, we just started. We realized the only way we were going to have small groups that multiplied was if we dived in headfirst and took some lumps and started learning some things. Sure, we made lots of mistakes, but each one was a learning experience that we want to share with you.

How to Use This Book

If you do not need to convince your church of the need for small groups, you can skip chapter 1 and go directly to chapter 2. From there you will find a step-by-step approach to birthing a small group system that has the potential to explode and multiply beyond your wildest dreams.

One word of caution: Our book is meant to be a guide, not a model. Don't copy us. Develop a process that will work in your setting.

Now to the process of starting a small group system that transforms lives!

CHAPTER ONE

THE NEED FOR CONNECTION

People are more disconnected today than ever before. What happened to the Ward and June Cleaver world where community and family was the very core of life? What happened to the neighborhoods of the 1950s where everyone on the street knew one another? What happened to the neighborhoods where kids would run and play without the fear of the kinds of things that feed a parent's worst fears?

The Situation: We're Disconnected

People were safer because they were connected to everyone. In times past we not only knew our neighbors but were also more of an active part of the community. What happened to the relationship parents had with their children's teachers, coaches, and principals? Why don't we know the local grocer or the local police officers anymore? What happened to the days when communities came together to celebrate with one another, care for one another, live life together, and protect one another?

You can probably add ten more "why's" that we haven't thought of, but you get the point. What happened to community?

We saw community happen during the weeks following 9/11. People from all over the U.S. came together in a display of community. But look at the U.S. now, just a few years later. We're once again a disconnected, fragmented nation. What was it about 9/11 that changed the way we acted toward one another, and if it can happen during a time like that, why doesn't it happen every day in our communities?

Community happened because we became connected. The events of 9/11 forced us to love our neighbors more than ourselves and reminded us that we are the community of the United States of America. The question now becomes, how do we stay connected? Clearly in the right situation community can happen. So then what are we doing or not doing that keeps community from happening every day?

In today's world people can live disconnected from others even while attending and serving in church.

We believe the problem starts with our families. Husbands and wives are becoming more disconnected. Most husbands and wives spend at least five days a week in the work environment separated from each other. If that much of our lives is spent apart then it is only natural for each person to build relationships apart from one another. Companies used to address this by having barbeques and parties to make sure their employees stayed connected. Unfortunately, that's pretty much a thing of the past. Since the two work experiences exist apart from each other, the situation creates a disconnection.

What about our kids and school? Remember when it seemed like we all went to one big school? It wasn't unusual for parents to know all the teachers and most of the kids. Today it's not unusual for each child in the family to go to a different school. It's almost impossible to create any relationships with the people at those schools because you're never there long enough before you head to your next stop.

What about the outside activities your kids do? How about the mom who has three or four kids and each one is involved in a different sport or school activity? She runs from one game, practice, or function to another, barely having enough time to get from place to place, much less enough time to build some lasting relationships at any of them.

What about our church lives? Unfortunately, in far too many cases Christians show up for church each weekend, sing, listen to a message, then head out to find Sunday lunch. They are hearing the Word of God, but are they really becoming a part of the church? Are they building Christ-centered relationships that extend outside the doors of the church?

How many men in the churches of today have other Christian men helping them grow and holding them accountable? Not enough. If those men aren't finding Christian fellowship, then they are most likely finding the other kind of fellowship, which usually leads down the wrong path.

Women, on the other hand, are more likely to be involved in things at church. They are building relationships through their involvement in the church, and that's great. But do their husbands and children know one another? Do these relationships exist outside of the church walls or the ministry in which they are serving?

But what about the men's groups that meet for breakfast and talk about things that men need to talk about? Do these men's wives and children know one another? Please understand that both of these things are wonderful and very much needed, but we question whether they create a community in the church.

Many Christians go to church every weekend and serve in the ministry that their hearts are drawn to. This is fantastic and churches couldn't run on weekends without the servant hearts of these fine people. But is this creating community? People can live their lives disconnected from others even while attending and serving in church if they're not careful.

Small Groups Are the Solution

So what do we do? Do we just accept things as they are and move on with our lives? Unfortunately, many people believe that's just the way things are, and they accept the status quo. We aren't willing to do that. So let's talk about the solution to our lack of community.

To put it simply, small groups are the church's solution to our disconnected lives.

Small Groups Provide Fellowship

Fellowship is one of the solutions to our disconnected world. The Bible is full of scripture that says we need fellowship. First

John 1:7 says, "But if we are living in the light, as God is in the light, then we have fellowship with each other, and the blood of Jesus, his Son, cleanses us from all sin." The Bible says we need fellowship. So what is fellowship?

The biblical definition of fellowship comes from the Greek word, *koinonia*, which means, "putting good deposits into one another." That definition implies that we have to be giving something to each other or pouring ourselves into each other's lives for fellowship to occur.

Many people believe that coming to church each weekend fills both the worship and fellowship roles. But if you look at the word "fellowship" as the Bible uses it, you see that it takes far more to meet the biblical standard of fellowship than visiting with people at church or going to lunch together after church. Biblical fellowship can only happen through real community where people pour their lives into one another.

So where can we get the biblical fellowship and community we have been talking about? At most of the thriving congregations in the U.S. you find all of this through small groups that meet in homes. Small groups are groups of no more than fifteen people that meet weekly or biweekly in homes throughout the community, sharing life together through a combination of fun, fellowship, Bible study, and prayer. A healthy and growing small group ministry will unite and connect your church in amazing ways.

Small groups are groups of no more than fifteen people that meet weekly or biweekly in homes throughout the community, sharing life together through a combination of fun, fellowship, Bible study, and prayer.

Most of the fast-growing, dynamic churches see small groups as an important part of their future growth because they are a great way to make sure their church stays connected relationally and continues to grow at the same time. Small groups may not grow a church, but nothing does more to retain the people who do attend worship over the long haul than effective small groups that provide community.

Small Groups Share Life Together

Fellowship is about sharing life together. Sharing life together means you belong to a group of people you know you can count on, and who can count on you, no matter what struggles you face. These kinds of relationships won't happen at worship.

When your congregation begins to share life together you will see the heart of your church change as your people begin to serve in ministries, sacrificially give of their financial resources, and care for one another. Not to mention you are building the largest pastoral care machine in existence. Small groups become the first line of personal care for the hurts and needs of the people in your church. People should join a small group *before* they need one.

Small groups should be about the application of God's Word to our daily lives through fellowship and discussion. When this happens real relationships are built. When you take relationships and multiply them like this you begin a domino effect, which will then end up in other areas of your church and spill out into the community. When this kind of connectedness happens, people begin to feel like the church is *their* church and not *the* church. When people begin to call the church their church, you really see the domino effect as people begin to serve in a ministry. When these same people start serving they create another new set of relationships in the church body.

Can you begin to see what can happen in your church through the relationships built in small groups? Small groups become a catalyst for a relationally connected church, ministry volunteers, and the leaders you will need to take your church to the next level.

Small Groups Change Lives

Simply put, small groups change lives better than any other ministry in the church. Listen to John's personal story of how God worked in his life through small groups.

If it were not for the Hometeam ministry (small group ministry) at Bay Area Fellowship I don't believe I would have found my calling to ministry. I went to my first Hometeam about three months after I started attending our church. I was always a person who thought I could do it alone and was not thrilled about the idea of opening up to a room full of strangers. I probably

5

would not have gone to a Hometeam if not for the encouragement of my friends Bill and Cathy. They made sure there was no way I could say no. When I said no, Cathy asked me if I were *chicken*, and gave that little cluck-cluck sound that she knew would hit me right in my prideful gut.

> *Small groups become the incubator in which new Christians are bathed in love and care until they blossom.*

They took me to a group led by a wonderful couple named Clint and Liana. This was a mixed group with three singles and four couples. I remember so clearly how welcomed I was made to feel. This was not a contrived welcome; it was genuine and not based on anything other than they were just glad I had come to the group. That group was the first tool God used to begin to lead me to the ministry.

The same Cathy who invited me to that Hometeam was also the person who invited me to Bay Area. So I am in the ministry because of her obedience to God. A couple of years later I became the interim children's pastor, and I hired Cathy to be my children's church coordinator. Later, I promoted her to children's director, and then she was promoted to children's minister by our lead pastor, Bil Cornelius. God worked this entire plan out through Clint and Liana's Hometeam.

> *Small group ministry is a team effort in which every person in the church committed to the vision works toward its success.*

Small Groups Are God's Plan for the Church

Let's look at another example of scripture that supports why your church needs a healthy and growing small group ministry.

> They worshiped together at the Temple each day, met
> in homes for the Lord's Supper, and shared their meals
> with great joy and generosity—all the while praising
> God and enjoying the goodwill of all the people. And
> each day the Lord added to their fellowship those who
> were being saved. (Acts 2:46-47)

The earliest Christians met in the Temple for their corporate worship experience, but then they would go to homes and continue to study and fellowship together. Worship and fellowship are separate experiences. Small group worship is never meant to replace your weekend service; it is meant to help make it better by supporting it. These are different parts of a walk with God, and when done right, make both parts better.

The Apostle Paul talks about his meetings in homes as well.

> When they arrived he declared, "You know that from
> the day I set foot in the province of Asia until now I
> have done the Lord's work humbly and with many
> tears. I have endured the trials that came to me from
> the plots of the Jews. I never shrank back from telling
> you what you needed to hear, either publicly or in
> your homes. I have had one message for Jews and
> Greeks alike—the necessity of turning from sin and
> turning to God, and of having faith in our Lord
> Jesus." (Acts 20:18-21)

Even the Apostle Paul, with his enormous ministry, still found time to go to people's homes for fellowship. The same should be true today of any leader of a small group system. It's amazing what happens when the leaders drop into a home group. It lets people know a pastor really cares about their group.

Before Moving Forward

One word of caution: Before you do anything, decide what your small groups are going to look like. It's critical that you build a small group ministry that is designed to reach into the mindset of the people who live in today's society. One of the biggest failures in small group ministries we've seen is they're patterned after antiquated models of modernity that worked well for past generations. This is a new generation of people who see the world in far different ways than our parents saw things. Don't assume you know what the mindset of today's society is. If need be, spend time researching these new generations before you get started. For suggestions see the endnote.[1]

> *The key is to be culturally relevant and biblically sound.*

We hope this chapter has shed some light on the benefits of a healthy small group ministry in your church. Not only will small groups relationally connect your church, but they will spill out into other areas too, such as giving and volunteers. If you feel like God is speaking to your heart, read on and we will share the nuts and bolts of how to actually begin the process of starting a new ministry or growing the existing ministry you have.

Now to the actual step-by-step process of beginning a small group system that multiplies and experiences explosive growth.

Coaching Time

Use your imagination and think about what God can do to change lives through your small group ministry.

- How many families attend your church?
- How many singles attend your church?
- How many of these people are connected to the church in some way other than the weekend service?
- How many have no connection except the weekend service?

Note

1. For more information on modernity and the new generations see Bill Easum, *Leadership on the OtherSide* (Nashville: Abingdon, 2000);

Stanley Grenz, *A Primer on Postmodernism* (Grand Rapids: Eerdmans, 1996); Kevin Ford, *Jesus for a New Generation* (Downers Grove, Ill.: InterVarsity, 1995); Jimmy Long, *Generating Hope* (Downers Grove, Ill.: InterVarsity, 1995); Lyle Schaller, *Discontinuity and Hope* (Nashville: Abingdon, 1999).

In the past, most people came to church with some form of church background. That's not the case today. Most people under the age of forty have not grown up in church. Without a foundation people usually won't begin to really worship and search for God until they feel accepted. We see it all the time as you see people move from the back row, where they were able to remain anonymous, to the front row, where they are beginning to change because they've made friends.

A healthy small group ministry must be designed to meet people where they are so they have a chance to begin to see hope again. People are coming, whether they know it or not at the time, to find relationships. Since we know that relationships are what people are seeking, we have created a ministry designed to fill that need.

Our antiquated systems no longer work. They weren't designed to reach people with little or no Christian experience in their lives. They were designed for people who came from a world where there was structure and absolutes. They were great models that worked well in their time, but like music, they need to change or we will lose a whole generation.

CHAPTER TWO

THE FIRST STEPS ARE CRUCIAL

Step One: Bring the Lead Pastor on Board
Step Two: Convince the Powers That Be

The ground work is over. Our goal now is to assist you in the birth or growth of your small group ministry. We want to make this so simple it can't fail. So don't skip a step throughout the rest of the book

Step One: Bring the Lead Pastor on Board

Both of us have had a lot of opportunities to work with pastors and leaders who are looking for help to get a small group ministry going. And one thing stands out: if the lead pastor isn't personally involved in the small group ministry and doesn't support it from the pulpit, small groups never reach their potential. We've never seen an exception! The church may become a church *with* a few small groups, but it never becomes a church *of* small groups. The participation of the lead pastor is the single most important thing you must have if you are going to have a strong small group ministry. It is your job as small group pastor or leader to get your lead pastor on board *before* doing anything else. You can talk about small groups all day, but it doesn't have the same impact as it does when your pastor talks about it once during worship. (Of course, if you are the lead pastor and the small group leader you must have the same level of commitment.)

> *If your pastor isn't totally committed to small groups and doesn't support them from the pulpit, your small groups will never reach their potential.*

So our first question for you is, "Have you sat down with your lead pastor and asked him or her to join you?" By the end of this book you should have the tools you need to show your lead pastor the benefits to your church of a healthy small group ministry. It's a partnership that will determine your level of success.

Lead Pastor Examples

Bay Area Fellowship's (BAF) small groups are successful and growing because the pastor (Bil Cornelius) makes sure he is constantly casting the vision for why people need to join one of our groups. Twice a year he does a series on small groups leading to a small group rally, which focuses the entire church on one goal, getting into a small group. At their last rally (2005) BAF assimilated over five hundred people into small groups in just one day. We'll talk about the rally in depth later and tell you exactly how to do it and how your church can benefit from this method.

Not only does BAF do the rallies but throughout the year the pastor works small groups into his messages. You can work a good point about small groups into almost any topic. Doing so keeps small groups front and center on the minds of everyone who attends our church.

Every Monday morning I (Bill) would look on my desk and find a stack of forms—one from each small group. The forms kept me up on what happened that week in each small group. The small group leaders were encouraged to use the back of the form to record any life changes that took place that week. When persons experienced a major life change, I would call them and congratulate them on making the most important decision of their life. I would tell them the next few months would be the most important days in their life and to feel free to call me or their small group leader for any reason. Then I would always say to them, "When you are ready to tell your story in worship, let me know and I will help you prepare." I was committed to the ministry of small groups because I knew it changed lives.

Step Two: Convince the Powers That Be

You may have a church system that requires the vote of a board. If so, your next task may be to sell them on the concept of small groups and the benefits to the church.

Although a healthy small group ministry has no downside, plenty of misconceptions about them exist, so be prepared to defend your presentation with scripture. The two biggest issues when talking with the powers that be are the relationship between Sunday school and small groups, and the purpose of small groups. Let's look at those two issues now.

Small Groups and Sunday School Aren't the Same?

Sunday school may be small groups, but they are Bible study-driven rather than fellowship-driven and life-transforming like small groups, and they are done on the church premises on Sunday morning instead of in homes. *If you only get one thing from this chapter, remember this: small groups are not Bible studies.* People go to Sunday school to do in-depth Bible studies, and people go to small groups for relationships and to feel connected and loved. Every small group that is pure Bible study usually fails. Of course, there is a Bible study aspect to small groups, but that isn't the primary focus. We're not against Bible study or Sunday school; they just are not the same thing as a small group.

The question you have to ask yourself is, Does God care more about us knowing the Bible cover to cover, or does God care more about us having an intimate personal relationship with him and with one another?

13

Let us be clear, we are in no way taking the Bible out of our small groups. Everything you do in small groups should be driven by God's Word. What we don't want to do is try to recreate Sunday school in homes, because it won't work. Most churches have 20-30 percent of their worship in Sunday school, and we are trying to create a small group ministry that involves 60-70 percent or more of the weekend attendance.

The key is to decide what you think will help someone grow closer to Christ—a combination of love, service, and fellowship, or just Bible knowledge. The study part of the group is designed to work relationally. When the teaching is done the rest of the study time is people talking about how what they just learned can be applied to their everyday lives. People want to know how to apply centuries-old concepts to their lives today. So the majority of time is spent talking about just that. When groups are working the way they are designed to, people are talking to one another about how they learned to apply God's principles to their lives. They are also telling stories about how not applying them has negatively affected their lives, which can actually be more powerful.

So don't take the Bible out of your groups—just don't make scripture study the focus. Again there isn't anything wrong with Sunday school or Bible studies. You don't even have to pick one or the other. The key is to make sure everyone involved knows both are good, but they're also different. If you're not careful in this situation you'll create an "us against them" mentality, and it will hurt both.

Some of you may be struggling with this concept, so here is an example of how small groups can change lives without becoming Bible studies. If you have a married couple who are having marital problems and are considering divorce, what would help them more, someone using scripture to tell them what God says about divorce, or another couple telling them how God saved their marriage and that they love God and each other more than they ever have?

Small groups are not Bible studies.

Small groups are about sharing life together and discovering how the love of God transforms hearts. In small groups, instead of talking about life, people do life. When real relationships are formed you will find that there is no subject that can't be talked about openly.

Deep Bible learning and focused scripture study has a place, but it's not in a small group. You should make sure there are plenty of Bible studies available for those who want to attend them, but make sure your small groups are relationship-driven, not Bible study-driven. We will remind you of this distinction again.

Don't think everything you have ever done in Sunday school is wrong; it just means small groups are different. If your church has had Sunday school forever and there is not a chance it is ever going away, that's okay too. Have Sunday school on Sunday, and start a small group ministry during the week. One will be the place where your people can do their Bible study, and the other can be the place where people can share life together. Please don't give up on your dream for this ministry because you are in a traditional church or have denominational hoops to jump through. There is no denomination or church style where small groups won't work. You just have to create a system that will work for you.

Relationships and Life Change Are the Goals

People are looking for relationships built around affinity. Affinity means that the people in the small group have something basic in common. Affinity is a starting point to try to put people in groups with other people who are in the same place in life. Some are looking for people with a like mind for God because that's who they want to hang out with, and others are looking to surround themselves with people who can help them make real life changes. Others are there because everything else they have tried in their lives just isn't working. But all of these reasons have something in common: they are relational, and they have affinity.

A healthy small group starts by building relationships with one another. Once those relationships are built, you can work on building a relationship with God. People won't even talk about the tough issues of life until they are comfortable with and feel loved by the group. When most people begin the journey with Christ they still don't *feel* like they are worthy of being a part of any group with Christians in it. They are still struggling with how

15

God can love them with all the mistakes of their past. So building the relationship is the first step toward life transformation.

Build Around the New Christian and the Unchurched

Everyone benefits from a small group but no one more than new believers or nonbelievers because they so desperately need to share life with other Christians who have gone before them in their life struggles. They don't know what the next step is, and many leave the church because the thought of a walk with God is overwhelming. By loving and accepting them just like they are, real trust is built. When that trust is built then life change through biblical principles will happen. If you skip the first part, the second part will never happen.

Go out of your way to fill your small groups with baby Christians and nonbelievers. Create groups that are welcoming to the person who is the farthest from God, not the closest. That's where life change happens. If you gear everything to the most spiritual members of your church the non-Christians in your church pay the price. Also, because the spiritually mature also matter to God, make sure you have plenty of Bible studies available throughout the year.

Small Groups Are Incubators of Faith

You must also keep in mind that fellowship is just part of what happens in healthy small groups. Sooner or later people have to be connected to God through Christ. Small groups should be incubators of faith. Incubators are warm, safe environments where premature babies are nourished into a sustainable life. That's what needs to happen in small groups. In today's world people need to belong *before* they believe. That's one of the primary reasons you need small groups: they give people a place to belong, to be accepted, and then to begin to grow. But they need to be able to grow without the push to join something before they are ready. Give people the space they need to belong, and you have a very good chance of introducing them to Christ. Please understand that a small group will fail if it's about nothing but fellowship and fun. It must also transform lives; so creating balance is the key. We will talk about this balance later.

Going Forward

"And every day, in the Temple and from house to house, they continued to teach and preach this message" (Acts 5:42). The early church began the first small group ministry to keep everyone connected and growing together. That's your ammo in trying to convince the powers that be. If you present it right you have a good chance of convincing your elders or pastors of the benefits of a healthy small group ministry.

Let us restate something that we said in chapter 1. All of the growing, vibrant, community-changing churches we know have small group ministries. We don't believe your church can continue to grow and remain healthy if it grows past your ability to stay relationally connected. If you don't stay connected as a church you will have people at worship who hardly know one another much less participate in one another's lives.

Pastor Bil Cornelius of Bay Area Fellowship says it best, "People don't want to go to a friendly church. They want to go to a church where they have friends." There's a big difference. One is a place where people say hello in passing, and the other is a place where people love you through the good and bad times.

I (John) was recently teaching our Discovering Spiritual Maturity class when a young woman offered an example of what small groups have meant to her family. She was new to the church and had attended only one small group meeting when her brother was killed. Later, after the group had ministered to her in this tragedy, she said, "They barely knew us, yet they loved us through our tough time." That family may go through life and never really remember any one thing they learned in a Bible study, but you can bet they will never forget the love of those awesome Christians during one of the toughest times of their lives.

Reflection Time

- Do you clearly understand the difference between small groups and Sunday school, and the role Bible study and fellowship plays in each one? If not, reread that section.

- If you have not done so, sit down with your pastor and see if he or she is really committed to developing a small group system.
- Do you understand that your pastor's full and complete support is crucial to the future success of the small group ministry?
- Have you laid out exactly what that means for your pastor?
- Are your plans and your pastor's plans the same?
- Do you understand that if your pastor's plans are different from yours, you need to change your plan?

CHAPTER THREE

MANAGING A SMALL GROUP SYSTEM

Step Three: Build a Small Group Management System

We debated whether to put this step here or later in the process. On the one hand we were afraid if we put it here it might seem overwhelming. On the other hand we didn't want anyone to go off half-cocked and wind up with too many groups and no clear way to manage them. So we decided to make the management system step three even though you won't need it in the beginning. We just think it's a good idea to have a system in place before you begin in case your small groups explode in numbers. What if God so blesses your ministry that in a few months you have more small groups than you can handle? If such growth happens, you'll be glad you took the time to decide on your system of management.

Remember, at first you may have to wear all of the hats described in the following pages. But in time, as the number of small groups grows, you will see the wisdom in having your management system in place before you begin.

So your next step is to build a system of management by creating levels of leadership and systems to keep the ministry growing.

The System of Management

Unlike many other systems in large churches, our system has fewer levels of leadership. Many of the systems we've seen have multiple levels of leadership based on a span of fives or tens. For example, five small group leaders have one leader above them, then five of those leaders report to one leader above them.

Our system is based on twenty-fives. Twenty-five small groups per coordinator, and twenty-five coordinators per director. When the ministry grows past the ability for the director to handle the numbers of coordinators, then you can break the ministry down and add directors as needed. As the ministry grows, you may need to add a director of young couples, a director of mature couples, a director of singles, and a director of affinity groups, which includes everything else. As the ministry grows you can easily break down the couples and singles by ages and add additional directors. Each of these groups can be run like individual small group ministries. With additional directors and coordinators you can grow this ministry to any size.

In the beginning your system might look like this.

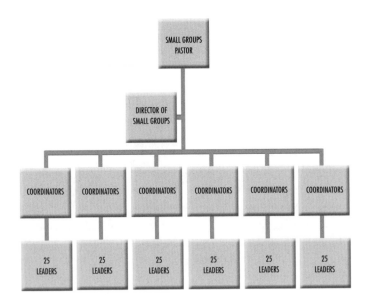

In time your system might look like this.

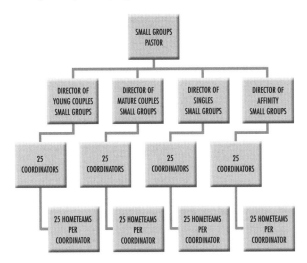

We prefer this more simple system because we want more of our best leaders leading small groups rather than overseeing the leaders of small groups. Our goal for small groups is life change. Overseers of leaders seldom change lives.

Let's look at this system from the bottom up so we can see how each level supports the others.

The Small Group Leader

The small group leader is the most critical leader in the whole system. These leaders are the people in the trenches doing the work of God and dealing with the tough life issues faced by the people in the church. Everything falls on their shoulders first, and the rest of the leadership exists to serve them.

The role of the small group leaders is to lead the people to a closer relationship with Christ by opening their homes and loving the people God has sent to them. Their goal is to change lives.

This is a big role in your church, and the people who are willing to do it need to know they are loved and supported or they will grow weary and quit. The worst thing that can happen in your ministry is for leaders to begin to feel unappreciated and uncared for. If you just send leaders out and forget about them, you'll look up and realize they've all quit. These leaders need encouragement, support, ongoing training, and appreciation. Here are the practical responsibilities of each small group leader. Small group leaders are required to:

- Open their homes and create a safe and comfortable atmosphere for life change.
- Be prepared to lead the small group a minimum of twice a month. Some groups meet weekly while others choose to meet biweekly. Anything less than twice a month will not create the community you are striving for.
- Contact the new people sent to them by their coordinator. Each leader is required to make multiple attempts (minimum of three) to contact each of the names and to keep a log of those calls for accountability.
- Live their lives in a way that honors God and represents the church well.
- Remember that their small group is not an autonomous organization operating on their own. Each group is an extension of the DNA of the church.
- Maintain regular two-way communication with their coordinator and ministry leadership. Part of the role of both coordinators and leaders is to maintain regular contact with one another so they are discussing any problems as well as how leaders are developing. A breakdown in communication here will cause a breakdown of the system. When coordinators and leaders have good solid relationships, they communicate regularly because the communication is done out of respect, not duty. Any system that involves volunteers must operate in the relational realm, because volunteers don't respond to duty the same way employees do. When this kind of relationship is established it builds real and trackable accountability into the system because coordinators keep the information gathered through this communication and are accountable to the pastor, lay leader, or director depending on how large the ministry is. This two-way communication is done in multiple ways—by e-mail, by phone, and in person.
- Give a monthly group health report to their coordinators. These reports consist of numbers of people attending, any

issues in the group, and potential new leader progress.
- Attend ongoing training and appreciation events.
- Encourage their members to join in events where the small group ministry is involved (special events, community action events, etc.).
- Sign a small group leader covenant saying they are committed to the vision of the ministry leadership, the church, and the rules and requirements of the role of small group leader. Each covenant must include the right of removal by the small group pastor. See appendix A.
- Champion the vision of the church and be willing to do whatever it takes to make that vision happen.

The Small Group Coordinator

Each small group coordinator oversees no more than twenty-five small groups. Their job is to encourage, train, love, and support their twenty-five leaders. This role is so time-consuming that in most cases it is the only role they have in the church.

These leaders are picked for their character, work ethic, leadership, and love of small groups. These leaders are lay pastors and carry all the responsibility of a pastor (keep in mind that we do not necessarily mean an ordained person when we use the word "pastor"). The role of coordinator is so vital that you need to take your best small group leaders and move them up to this role.

Let's define the role of the small group coordinators and talk about each of the responsibilities they have in overseeing their twenty-five groups.

Small group coordinators are required to:

- Make sure their groups are healthy and multiplying.
- Deal with any pastoral problems that may occur, as well as conduct ongoing training and make sure each leader in their group feels supported and cared for.
- Attend the monthly meeting with the small group pastor and director. In this meeting each coordinator is required to bring a small group health report on each group they oversee. The report consists of an overview of any problems or concerns, a list of names of people being prepared and trained for multiplication and their progress, and which groups need people

assigned to them. In this meeting each group is discussed and solutions and plans are made to meet the specific needs of the individual groups. This is also a time for praise and discussion of the real life-change stories from these groups. One of the tools you can use to cast vision for small groups is video testimonies. We will talk in depth about this later, but we find the people for those video testimonies in these meetings.

- Make sure the system of getting people into small groups is working the way it was designed. Each new name received should go to the church office first and then be passed on to a coordinator. Once a name leaves the office of the pastor it is the responsibility of the coordinators to make sure that person is called and invited to join a group. In a moment we will show you the system that each coordinator is expected to follow and track.

- Know each of their leaders on a personal level and oversee the spiritual growth of the group and its leadership. They are required to make sure each of their groups is healthy and multiplying.

- Visit their groups two to three times per year. This allows each coordinator to personally assess the health of each group and to build strong personal relationships with each of the leaders as well as those who are attending the groups.

- Have their leaders in their own homes one or two times per year. This allows them to continue to build personal relationships and to do ongoing leadership training with their leaders. This requirement is time-consuming, which is why you should keep the groups to no more than twenty-five per coordinator. If you have the right person or persons in this role, this requirement will be fun and exciting, not a burden. If visiting these groups and having leaders in their homes is a burden, replace that coordinator.

- Be completely loyal to DNA of the church. Coordinators are required to maintain regular contact with the pastor's office and the director of small groups.

- Be a member of the church. They are required to attend weekly church services and must be committed to biblically tithing to support the vision of the church.

- Sign a covenant making a commitment to the role as it is defined by the ministry leadership. This covenant includes the right of removal by the small group pastor for any reason determined necessary.

The role of small group coordinator is an extremely high trust role and should not be filled unless the pastor is comfortable with the persons being chosen. The system will break down if you don't have the right people in place. You have to trust your coordinators to do what they have agreed to do. Pick your best people for this role and be willing to remove anyone who doesn't meet the requirements.

Director of Small Groups

This role will become necessary later as your ministry grows. The director's primary role is to lead, train, and grow the small group coordinators. It is the director's role to oversee ongoing coordinator training and to make sure that the coordinators are doing their job as it is defined in their covenant. The director's role is to make sure the coordinators have picked and trained the right people and to oversee the job they are doing. This role needs to be filled by one of your best small group leaders who became one of your best small group coordinators. This is the highest trust role in this system because this person answers directly to the pastor and will assist him or her in dealing with the daily problems and issues of the ministry. This role must be filled with the potential successor to the small group pastor in the event that the pastor leaves or is moved to another position. This person should be so effective that he or she challenges everyone to have to step up his or her leadership every day. This person has the authority to make decisions on their own and has the discernment to know when to make those decisions and when to go to the small group pastor with those decisions.

This is a role you don't need until the ministry gets fairly large. Until then most of these responsibilities can be performed by the small group coordinators who report directly to the small group pastor. You will know you need this person when, as the small group pastor, you realize that your time is being overwhelmed with the day-to-day issues, and you are no longer focused on vision and leadership. Be careful because this will happen before you know it, and you'll look back and realize you kept this ministry from growing because all you were doing was reacting to the day-to-day issues.

The Small Group Pastor or Leader

In the beginning this person might be the pastor of the church or a lay person (we are not necessarily using the word "pastor" to refer to an ordained person). But as soon as you can, hire someone who feels called to and passionate about small group ministry. The sooner you do this the more effective your small groups will become.

The role of the small group pastor is to create the system and cast the vision for the ministry and to motivate people to want to be a part of the system. This person must believe God can do anything and must set goals that reflect that kind of faith. If the small group pastor sets goals that he or she can figure out how to get to, you will have created a small group ministry that will be held back by its leader's lack of vision and faith.

The small group pastor is the key to the success of the entire system working like it is designed. If you're a senior pastor or someone in a role to pick the small group pastor, please make this decision wisely. Don't hire someone just because he or she has a seminary degree and wants to work in your church. Hire someone you know is called to and passionate about small groups. One of the best ways to do this is to hire from within. That way you already know the person's heart. Start by giving people a leadership role and watching how they handle it. If they handle the initial role well then start adding responsibilities and see what kind of fruit they are producing.

Every ministry has its problems in the beginning. Groups will fail, and there will be struggles—especially if you don't begin with a full-time leader, so don't let that discourage you. Be prepared for the ministry not to take off and grow until you have that person, and be willing to wait on God to reveal him or her to you.

However, don't let the lack of a full-time pastor of small groups keep you from getting started. Find honest, hard-working lay leaders with a heart for small groups, and let them create a ministry. Most small group ministries will begin with lay leaders doing almost everything. During this time be looking for that right person to lead the ministry full time. The other levels of leadership will come along as the ministry grows.

If the ministry already exists and the church leadership is ready to find a full-time leader, look at the best small group leader in the ministry. You will know who it is because his or her group will have multiplied numerous times and he or she will be raising up leaders right and left. This person is the one everyone talks about when they think of a leader. When you find this person, whose character and walk with God matches his or her leadership, offer the job. This may or may not be your full-time ordained pastor of the future, but we wouldn't put someone in that role who doesn't have that potential. If your church polity allows it, be prepared to ordain this person for the role he or she already loves and is prepared by God for, recognizing that "God doesn't call the equipped, he equips the called." Some truly amazing things will happen in your church when you realize that the called are not always seminary-trained. When you hire from within, you hire loyalty, and nothing is more important.

I (John) am a living, breathing example of God calling someone to the ministry and equipping them for the job. I didn't come with much experience or a seminary degree, but I came with a love and passion for small groups and the lives that I knew could be changed through them. One hundred seventy small groups later, I think it's fair to say that God must have had something to do with my calling or I couldn't have accomplished this because I sure didn't come with anything except a crystal-clear calling from God.

When choosing your small group pastor it's important to make sure the person has the personality to spread that passion. Be careful here, because many people with passion aren't gifted at sharing it. Your small group pastor needs to have a personality that people are drawn to and the leadership that people will follow.

We have talked about this role last, but it is actually the first choice you need to make, so make it wisely because the ministry will live or die by this choice. Your small group pastor is the leader, and the future success of the ministry will be determined by his or her character, passion, vision, creativity, and leadership. The small group pastor must create and cast a vision that challenges every single person all the way down to the small group attendee. This person must be completely and totally loyal to the senior pastor.

When looking at this system, the most important thing to look for as you are filling these leadership roles is loyalty. Loyalty to the vision of the church, and loyalty to the small group leadership and its vision for the ministry. Fill these roles with a bunch of competent people you love, trust, and believe in and the system will work great.

Don't Be Afraid to Hold People Accountable

As the small group pastor/leader you are responsible for making sure the system works long term. Your pastor needs to help here through the Sunday morning worship, but you also must stay on top of the system. You must hold the leaders accountable to what they agreed to accomplish when they began. Later we will talk about what they agree to do. Let's face it, either you will lead your leaders, or they will lead you. Too many lives are at stake for you to let your system run amok.

We don't agree with a lot written on accountability or reporting. Times have changed, and so has the way you hold people accountable. When I (Bill) was a pastor, accountability was achieved through a massive paper-trail reporting system. It worked then; it doesn't today.

Early on I (John) required leaders to send in weekly reports letting me know everything that was going on in their group. I looked up one day and realized I was spending more time chasing down the reports than reading them. I also realized that the constant hounding was actually hurting my relationship with my leaders. Upon real and honest reflection I realized the reporting was my attempt to maintain total control of the ministry. I also realized that my desire to control was the very thing that was keeping the ministry from thriving.

Listen up: health comes through relationships, not rules. Today, you hold people accountable through developing solid relationships. I (John) no longer have my leaders turn in reports.

The question most people will ask is, "How do you make sure your groups are healthy without regular reporting?"

First, you need to know that nothing that is ever turned in on a report will tell you anything about the health of a group. If you want to know about the health of your groups, build solid relationships with each of your leaders. Healthy groups don't come from a lot of training or good curriculum. Healthy groups come from healthy leaders.

The first twenty-five groups I (John) had were extremely healthy. They were healthy because I was personally mentoring each group leader. I visited their groups regularly and had them in my home. I took them to lunch and hung out with them. They knew I cared about their group and that I was there for them no matter what. They loved being leaders, their excitement was contagious, and the people in their groups were growing because of that excitement. Again the health came from our relationship, not from me pounding them to fill out a form.

I also realized that twenty-five leaders were about as many relationships as I could handle and keep the quality the same. So I created the next level of leadership so those same kinds of relationships would continue.

Small group coordinators have the same responsibility that John had in the beginning. Their primary role is to build healthy and strong relationships with the leaders they oversee. They visit each of their groups two to three times per year. They have group leaders in their homes for a time to be served, since they are always serving others, and they stay in regular contact through phone and e-mail. They are personally mentoring each of the leaders in their group, and they are required to report all of this information to the office of the small group pastor.

You need monthly coordinator meetings. Coordinators must commit to attend these meetings unless there is an emergency (have them sign a covenant to attend). Require them to bring a monthly health report on all of their groups. The report details any problems with people in groups, any problems with group leaders, a group attendance report that includes a list of groups who need people assigned to them, and a regular report of who is being prepared for leadership and their progress. There is no standard form for this because I have found that people like to do things their own way. The form is less important than the content.

If coordinators create and maintain healthy and real relationships with their leaders and if you maintain healthy and real relationships with your coordinators, the ministry will be healthy. This may sound like a pipe dream to some, but it's not. We can tell you without a shadow of a doubt that it works.

Your whole system needs to be driven by people loving and being loved—transforming relationships. Groups focus on relationships so that they are healthy. Leaders are healthy because of the relationships they have with coordinators, not from reporting. And while coordinators are required to report, they will become some of your most trusted and loyal leaders. Add to all of that good curriculum and fun, and you will see real life-change happening in groups all around you.

Coaching Time

- Before starting out, take some time to design the management system that you feel will best suit the future of your small group ministry.
- If you are the lead pastor, before starting your small groups or even finding a leader, give some thought to how you want your small groups to function and what you want them to achieve.
- Spend time praying that God will send the right person your way, and keep your eyes open for that person.
- If you are in charge of finding the right person to lead your small group ministry, have you considered that he or she may be right under your nose?
- Have you considered that he or she may be your best small group leader?
- For the ministry to thrive, the person you choose needs to have a passion for small groups, not just a passion for ministry.

CHAPTER FOUR

MULTIPLYING SMALL GROUPS

Step Four: Pray for and Create a Culture of Multiplication

The multiplication of small groups is the single most important element of every healthy small group ministry that has longevity. From the beginning the DNA of your small group system must hinge on the multiplication of every small group. Multiplication should be a part of the DNA of every small group ministry and should be taught to small group leaders as a key element of their leadership role. Failure to understand this step is usually fatal to any small group system.

A number of things happen to small groups that don't multiply, and none of them are good:

- They eventually become unhealthy, and most of them die.
- The atmosphere for life change dissipates because there's no one new in the group.
- Groups often become closed where no one new is invited in, and if new people do show up they feel like outsiders and don't return.
- The groups become boring because everyone has heard everyone's story more than once.
- They often become a place to criticize the church and its leadership, and when that happens, it's like a virus that works its way into many areas of the church. Every small

group that we have seen that began to criticize the church and its leadership was one where the same people had been together for too long.

Creating a Culture of Multiplication

So how do you create a small group ministry with a DNA of multiplication?

Multiplication isn't easy because it goes against the very thing you are trying to create—community. So you must train your leaders to talk about multiplication in the small group from day one and to continually cast that vision on a regular basis. If a leader talks about it all the time, when it's time to multiply, everyone will be expecting it to happen.

Life change seldom happens in small groups that don't multiply.

Sounds simple, doesn't it? Well, it's not! You can rest assured multiplication won't happen on its own. The ministry leader is the key to making multiplication work in a small group ministry. It needs to be part of your ministry's vision and goals, and like any vision, you must recast it over and over.

Because having a system in which small groups multiply regularly isn't easy to create, some people reading this might be thinking, "Well that's easy for you because you started yours that way, but I'll never get mine to change." Not true; neither one of us started our small group ministry that way because we didn't know small groups had to multiply to remain healthy. We had to clean up our mess after we figured that out. So you can change your small group system too. It won't be easy, but you can do it.

Both of us have had the honor of working with many pastors who have had to change the thinking in their groups and did so successfully. All of them would tell you it's not easy, but it can be done. See the endnote for a short list of some of the churches where we've seen this happen.[1]

So let's start from square one and talk about the steps you can take to begin to create small groups that multiply. Where do you start and what do you do to keep the small groups multiplying?

Leadership Training

Leaders need to be taught from the beginning that one of the primary goals of their ministry is the multiplication of their group within the first year. Don't make the mistake of thinking you can teach this basic later. Far too many small group leaders put little or no emphasis on training their leaders. This is a huge mistake. If you bypass this training you send leaders out to do small groups however they feel is best instead of carrying out the DNA of the church and the small group ministry. You want to lead a church with explosive growth, and that doesn't happen if everyone goes off and does whatever they want to do. If the small group leaders don't exercise the DNA, which is multiplication, you will be creating an unhealthy ministry and the consequences are going to be painful.

> *Embedding small group multiplication into each leader is an essential element in a healthy small group system.*

By making multiplication part of your original leader training, you are creating the multiplication DNA from day one. Every person leaves leader training knowing that multiplying his or her group is a vital part of leading it. All new leaders know that they are expected to talk about multiplication on day one of their group. If they don't want to do this, they don't lead a small group. It's that simple. Being the leader means it's your job to create and set the vision for the ministry, and it also means that anyone who wants to lead a small group must follow that vision. One of the biggest mistakes we have seen is pastors who are allowing small group leaders to dictate to them what they will and won't do. This simply must not happen, and if a leader will not follow your vision, remove that person.

Recasting the Vision for Multiplication

It's great that the vision was cast for multiplication during leader training, but don't expect that to be enough. Multiplication of groups is tough work, and like any tough task it takes continuous effort. Here are some ways to continue to recast the vision for multiplication.

- Continually seek to grow the number of new leaders being trained by your small group leaders. I (Bill) have never seen a small group system grow any faster than it can produce and train new leaders.
- Use e-mail to do ongoing leader training, and ask your leaders if they are preparing to multiply their group. Ask for specific rather than general answers concerning issues such as how they are doing finding and equipping someone to take their place.
- Hold ongoing leader training a few times a year, and ask all leaders whether they have someone they are preparing to hive off and start a new group. During the training have a card sitting on a table and ask them to write down the names of potential leaders so you can follow up.
- Empower and train the coordinators to do training in two ways—to visit each group at least three times per year and to have their leaders in their homes several times per year.
- Meet monthly with the coordinators to review how the small groups are doing.
- Host a leader appreciation dinner three or four times a year where you thank your leaders for their commitment to the ministry. Ask them who they are preparing for leadership; talk about the importance of multiplication; and remind them of the commitment they made during leader training. Have a great meal and a small appreciation gift for each of the leaders. Pastors, don't miss this opportunity, because having your leaders all together and telling them how much you love and appreciate them is powerful.
- Every time you see small group leaders, ask whether they have anyone they are preparing to start another group.
- Send a card of thanks to each leader, and while you're at it, ask them if they are working on someone to start a new group.
- Go and visit a group, and while you're there ask everyone in the room if anyone is ready to think about starting a new

group. This will help reinforce your small group leader's attempt to raise up new leaders. Three or four times a year take potential leaders' names and follow up with their leaders.

- Identify leadership potential in people at church, and ask them to lead a group. Do you have any idea what it means to people for you to think they are leadership material? You'll never know who will lead if you don't ask.

- Ask every former small group leader to step up again. Some may have quit for a reason that no longer exists and have been waiting to be asked again. Some may have just not thought about it in a while and need to be asked again.

- Create a handout that says something like "Become a small group leader" and insert it in the weekly bulletin or hand it out to every person who comes through the door during services. Then have a meeting where the people who filled it out find out what leading a group is all about.

In short use anything you can think of to make sure that you are always recasting the vision for small group multiplication. If *you* don't make it happen, it won't happen!

Multiplication is not easy, so don't think it will happen just because you talk about it. Multiplication is an ongoing effort, and when the ideas you're using quit working, come up with some new ones. You'll never be able to take time to relax and see the fruits of your work if your church is growing. In a growing church your small groups will always be behind the curve. The more groups you add, the harder it gets to keep the multiplication DNA alive. And if you have one person trying to make that happen it will most likely fail. That's why you need to create a system that makes sure each group has someone over them who can do everything we have talked about in this chapter in order to keep groups multiplying. Success can be achieved with the multiple levels of leadership we talked about in chapter 3.

Raising up New Leaders: New Leader Preparation Requires a System

When it comes to raising up new leaders, it's important to make sure you have a system. You can't just hope this will happen, because it won't. The future growth and health of your small group ministry depends on your ability to find leaders to lead new groups.

In the beginning, when the ministry is small, the pastor or lay leader's personal involvement in the process of producing new leaders is key. As the ministry leader the most important thing you must do is create a DNA of multiplication. Every leader must be encouraged to raise up other leaders so the small groups can multiply.

All leaders should clearly understand their role in raising up new leaders before they ever have their first meeting. With the multiplication vision cast, the next thing you need to do is put in place a system of accountability so you can track results. Let's look first at a small group system where the pastor or lay leader is the only leader.

- Have leaders provide a list of potential new leaders in their groups within the first few months of starting their group. These are potential new leaders so the list is subject to change.
- Have leaders provide monthly or bimonthly updates on the progress of each person and an update if names have changed.
- Set time goals so leaders are working on your schedule, not their own. Setting goals addresses the basic human nature of waiting until the last minute to do something.
- Provide ongoing training and encouragement to existing leaders so they can be successful in reproducing their leadership in others.
- Never miss an opportunity to recast the multiplication DNA vision.
- Use other forms of communication to talk about multiplication. Use things like e-mail, mailers, newsletters, and personal visits both to groups and privately with leaders. Take time to have a meal with leaders. Don't underestimate the value of spending private and personal time with your leaders.

When the ministry begins to grow you must put in place other levels of leadership or the system will fail. We call this next level of leadership small group coordinators. We talked about this group in chapter 3. This level is necessary when you get to a maximum of twenty-five small groups. We have found that the ability to care properly for each individual group diminishes past that point.

The roles change when the next level of leadership is in place. Coordinators take on a role similar to that of the pastor or lay leader when they were the only person available. They become the lay pastor or overseer of their twenty-five groups. The primary lay leader or pastor at this point will begin to focus on leading and training coordinators, as well as vision-casting and the overall health and future of the ministry. Here is the role of the coordinator in reproducing future leaders.

- Coordinators are responsible for continuing to recast the vision for multiplication with each of the leaders in their group. This is to be done in the same ways that the pastor or lay leader did it before this level of leadership existed.
- Each coordinator is responsible to keep a list of potential new leaders from each group and their progress.
- Coordinators are responsible to make sure the time goals set by the ministry leadership for raising up new leaders is met.
- Coordinators will be responsible for ongoing leadership training and development with each leader in their group. This is critical in preparing leaders to reproduce themselves in others.
- Coordinators are responsible to attend monthly meetings with the pastor or lay leader of the ministry. In each of those meetings coordinators are required to provide a group health report, which will include a list of people being prepared for leadership and their progress. This creates a system of accountability so progress on potential new leaders can be tracked.

This system works when each level of leadership clearly understands his or her role. When leaders know that part of the role of leadership is to produce new leaders, they are more likely to do it. When coordinators know that they are responsible to recast the multiplication DNA vision, they are more likely to do it. When all levels of leadership understand that they are required to provide a list of potential new leaders and their progress to the leaders they are under, they are more likely to do it.

The key to multiplying groups is to create the multiplication DNA or mindset in your ministry. It's never easy to reproduce leaders, but you can be assured to fail if you don't have a plan. A successful plan is one where every person in the ministry, no matter what level they are on, knows that reproducing their leadership in others is the key to the ministry's growth and health.

In trying to develop new leaders, there are two very costly mistakes you can make: First, the leader can try to ensure that everything is perfect; and second, the leader can allow his or her level of leadership to be the standard for others. The problem with the first mistake is volunteers never start out anywhere near perfect, and having that as a standard means that few people will measure up. The problem with the second mistake is that even the best leaders were like everyone else who is new to the role. They learned as they led. In raising up new leaders, current leaders must never forget what it was like when they first started. If you expect too high a standard for leadership, you will never find enough leaders to keep up with your growing church. You will work your way through all of the truly gifted teachers in your church in the first twenty-five or thirty groups, and then you're stuck. The standard should be character, not knowledge. Never forget this. You can train skills; you can't train character.

Your Charter

Whatever you do, make sure your groups multiply. It's healthy for the ministry, healthy for leaders, and healthy for the church. If your groups don't multiply it will create more trouble than benefit. However, if you commit to creating a multiplying and growing small groups ministry you will be creating a machine for life-change that will shape the future of your people and your church.

Coaching Time

- Is it clear to you that the multiplication of your small groups is essential to a healthy small group system?

- How are you planning on instilling the virtue of multiplication into your leaders?
- Have you decided on how you are going to train your leaders?

Note

1. The Connection Church in Kyle, Texas, and Crossroads UMC in Pittsburgh are just two examples.

CHAPTER FIVE

FINDING NEW LEADERS: PART ONE

Step Five: Find Effective Small Group Leaders
Step Six: Develop Several Levels of Leadership

L et's assume the senior pastor and board members are convinced of the need for small groups, you have developed your management system, and you are absolutely convinced about the necessity of multiplication. (If you already have a small group ministry and these things aren't already accomplished, that probably explains why the ministry isn't reaching its potential.) So where do you go from here?

Step Five: Finding Effective Small Group Leaders

The fifth step is finding effective, loyal leaders. As long as you lead a growing, multiplying small group system, finding leaders will be your single biggest loss of sleep.

So, where do you begin?

You Begin by Asking People to Lead

Nothing is more important in a small group ministry than simply asking people to lead a small group. Failure to remember this will always result in the failure of your small group ministry. It is as simple as that.

As your ministry grows, the time will come when you won't be able to continue to personally ask the people you know to lead your small groups. But in the beginning you making the ask is *the* best way to make sure you start off with solid leaders and build a firm foundation for the ministry. As the ministry grows larger the job of finding and encouraging new leaders will be shared by the other levels of leadership we talked about in chapter 3.

If you don't ask people to lead a small group, the right people seldom lead. So never be afraid to ask people to lead.

Your church is full of people who are waiting to be asked to serve; so ask and ask and ask. As you ask people to lead your groups, you'll find some will be honored that you would even think of them, while others will be a bit freaked out because they don't feel qualified. We'll talk about that freaky feeling later.

Be prepared to hear lots of "Nos," but don't be surprised when you also hear "Yes!" As the leader you are going to have to ask for leaders over and over, so before you ask anyone, start by praying for the people you are getting ready to ask so that God can prepare their hearts. They are all just people with all the same doubts and fears that all of us have, so lift them up and encourage them.

The single most important thing you look for in any leader is character. If a person has character, everything else is teachable. Here are some keys to look for in potential small group leaders.

Look for Humble People

Look for humble people who love God with all their hearts and are trying their best to grow closer to him, humble people who don't think they know enough about the Bible to be good leaders; who aren't afraid to say, "I don't know, but I'll find out"; whose experience in their own small groups has changed their lives so much that they want to share that joy with others; who know they can't lead a small group without God's help.

Humble leaders have a heart for God. Let them know they are being asked for that reason and that nothing else matters to you. If you start with a person who has a true heart for God, regardless of where they think they are in their walk, you will never lose. You can give them the training, but you can't give them a heart for God.

> **Nothing beats humble, loyal leaders who have a heart for God, no matter how skilled they are.**

Some of the best small group leaders either of us have had started with very little knowledge of the Bible and were fairly new to their walk with God. They realized early on that they had to rely on God and others. They became great leaders because they loved God with all their hearts and were willing to do anything God asked them to do. Let them know you chose them for that very reason. Tell them you believe in them and that you know they will make great leaders.

Look for Loyal People

As a leader of your small group ministry you must raise up leaders who are willing to follow you. Loyalty is one of the things that you must expect, especially when you put together your leadership team. You won't be able to grow it if your leaders are not loyal to the vision.

Don't ever let your vision from God get hijacked. If you're not careful you will wake up one day and not recognize the ministry you created. If you're called by God to lead the ministry, then lead it. You can't lead a growing and vibrant ministry by taking a vote on every issue. Being a leader means you have to make leadership decisions and be willing to stand up and take responsibility for them whether they work or fail.

Give Anyone a Chance to Be a Small Group Leader, Except Coordinators

You can never know for sure about people until you give them a chance. We have some great leaders that we gave a chance, thinking they would fall flat on their faces—and they didn't. You will miss some great leaders by not giving them a chance to succeed. Don't let them lead so they would fail; pray that they will succeed. If you're not willing to do this then don't let these person lead.

Small group coordinators are very different. Such a high trust is placed in them you must set the standard of leadership higher. Here are the things to look for in a small group coordinator: just magnify everything we've said above about what to look for in a leader.

Helping People Not to Be Afraid to Lead

People often feel unqualified to lead for many reasons, but often the real reason is fear. Fear of not knowing the answer to a question posed by a member of the group; fear of never having led anything before; fear of the title "leader"; fear that no one will talk and they will have to carry it all; fear that no one will come; fear that they aren't good enough Christians to lead; the list goes on and on. These are real fears, and most of the people you ask will have some or all of them. So how do you convince people with these kinds of fears to step up and lead?

The best thing you can do is encourage them. They need to know that:

- you see something in them that they don't see in themselves;
- they don't have to be super Christians for God to be able to use them;
- they have a support system in place to help them with any problems they might have along the way;
- no one has all the answers, so they don't need to either;
- God uses servants like small group leaders to change people's lives;
- God will grow and change their life also through their commitment to leadership.

From finding leaders, to growing and multiplying your groups, to keeping the groups you have healthy, nothing is more important than the encouragement you give to your leaders.

Sometimes you will start a new group and for some reason no one comes to it. Usually the leaders blame themselves or think God didn't want them to do this. This is a time to be an encourager and let them know that if they pray about this and hang in there, you will do everything you can do to get their group going. I (Bill) used to approach a failing leader this way: "Tell me where I failed to equip you, because I know you have what it takes to do this. So let's both work on this together."

Releasing Small Group Leaders

If you are careful in your selection and you coach them well, it's not often that a small group leader has to be released. In most cases it has to do with a failure of character or disloyalty to the church or the ministry. In each case it's very important to try to help a leader grow and heal. You may have to remove a leader for a period and let healing take place. Other times you may just put in place some steps they must follow and if they follow them they can stay in their role.

When making this decision it's important to look at the person's history. Is this an ongoing failure or did a good leader simply letting sin get the best of them?

We've not found a good way to release a leader. You will rarely go into a discussion of this kind knowing what the outcome will be. Watch how people being confronted handle your confrontation, because that says more about where they are with God than anything else. But right is always right no matter how hard it is or who gets hurt by it.

Having to release a coordinator is a major issue. Coordinators are held to a much higher level of accountability, so they also must be dealt with differently. Their failure hurts every group they oversee, so the standards are higher and the consequences stronger.

When leaders need to be removed then you just have to remove them and the quicker the better. Once your intuition tells you to release them, do it. Don't wait.

However, before you go around releasing people, make sure you have accountability in your life. Never make one of these decisions lightly, and always talk it over with other pastors on your staff so you can make sure you're right about what you're about to do. But remember, part of leadership is doing the tough things no one else wants to do.

Step Six: Develop Several Levels of Leadership

As the number of leaders and small groups grows you will come to the point when you begin to feel overwhelmed. When you start feeling that way it's time to develop the next levels of leadership we talked about in chapter 3. Developing these additional levels of leadership is a very important step in managing a healthy small group ministry, and there are two key issues to think about when doing it.

- Timing is key in setting up these new leadership levels. One of the biggest mistakes I (John) made was waiting until I was completely overwhelmed before I set up the next level of leadership called coordinators. Don't wait until you have problems to do this. Set up your next level before you feel like you need it.
- Picking the right people is extremely important. We will talk about this in detail later, but don't just go find the first warm and willing bodies and put them in this position. The key here is to begin working on this prior to the need so that you can take your time and pick these leaders carefully and prayerfully. The wrong choice here will cause more problems than it will solve.

So how do you find the next level of leadership? These leaders will come from the best of the best of your small group leaders. You'll know who they are because they are the leaders who have led healthy and *multiplying* small groups. They will be the beginning of the creation of your inner circle of leaders whom you will turn to for their advice and ideas as you grow the small group ministry.

Be smart as you fill these roles. These must be loyal and smart leaders who are on board with the vision and are willing to be a part of a team. Trust them, listen to them, and let them have the freedom to be honest and speak their hearts at all times. But when the meetings are over and you walk out the door, you need to know they are with you even if everything didn't go exactly the way they thought it should.

Because great small group leaders are so hard to find, one of the hardest things you will have to do is pull some of them out of their successful groups and move them to the new levels. It will eat at you because they are so good at what they are doing and their groups are the ones that are multiplying all the time. But these leaders are more valuable to the future of the ministry if they are put in a position where they can train other leaders. Most great leaders will replace themselves before they leave their group anyway, and the group will stay together and be healthy without them.

Your Role Begins to Change

As you develop the two new levels of leadership (coordinators and director) your role as the leader of the ministry begins to change. Your main job at this point will be to pour your heart and soul into your coordinators (first new level) and let them do the same to the small group leaders they oversee. Making this shift could be a tough role change for you, because it requires you to step back and let your leaders lead, which also means giving them the freedom to fail. We know it's hard to let go, but they will never become great leaders if you don't.

Moving On

We will share more on your role later, but for now just realize that in the beginning you fill all three of the roles outlined in chapter 3. But as the ministry grows you must let go and develop great leaders in these positions or the small group movement will stagnate at the level you are able personally to maintain. No one with a kingdom mind-set would let that happen.

Coaching Time

- Keeping the attributes of a great small group leader in mind, begin a list of the people who come to mind. Look over the qualities of a great small group leader carefully. By nature you will tend to lean toward the people you think are the most spiritual. The most important quality to look for is character; everything else is teachable.

- Start praying for these people, and when the time is right ask them to join you as a small group leader.
- As people from your list begin to lead small groups keep a list of those who excel in leading the group. By excel we mean they always reproduce leaders and multiply their group. These are candidates for coordinators or director.
- How do you feel about the time when you have to release some of your present responsibilities to your coordinators? Do you need some help in making this transition? If so, what is it and who can help you?
- Once you have small groups make sure those leaders understand that one of their primary roles is to raise up new leaders. The future growth of the ministry depends on it.
- Be prepared to have to give up some of your best leaders when creating new levels of leadership. They are your best leaders because they have the highest character, loyalty, and commitment.

CHAPTER SIX

FINDING NEW LEADERS: PART TWO

Step Seven: Avoid Problem People

When looking for people to lead your groups, you'll hear many excuses why someone can't lead: I don't know the Bible well enough. My life isn't where it needs to be yet. I'm just not ready yet. I've made too many mistakes in my life for God to be able to use me like this. I don't have enough time. My house isn't big enough.

In this chapter we'll talk about why most of these people, with all their excuses, often make the best small group leaders. That may seem strange to you, but realize that most of their excuses are based on fear of the unknown and actually show humility.

Personality Types to Avoid

As we go through this list remember exceptions always exist. As we look at each personality type remember that true humility and a heart for God can change anyone.

The Biblical Scholar

Most of the time when self-professed biblical scholars want to lead a small group they come into the process with the idea that they are intellectually above others in the group because they know scripture so well. They are intent on teaching biblical principles to a group of people who need to know the Bible like they do. They want to "take them deeper." We laugh when we hear that because what is deep enough and who decides what the standard of depth is? The truth is, Jesus is the standard, not some people who put themselves at some elevated status. If Jesus is the standard then none of us are deep enough. With these people it usually isn't about the ministry, it's about them.

The Born Leader

Most born leaders have never had to rely on others for anything. They have accomplished great things in their lives and have never had to ask anyone for help. These folks are generally good people with fantastic work ethics. Their problem is they are too self-sufficient. A small group can only be a great small group if the person leading it recognizes that the success of the group depends on whether he or she is willing to lean on God. One of the toughest challenges for born leaders is to surrender self to God. So sometimes these people just can't ask for help.

The strongest leader without a humble heart for God is a problem you're better off without.

Here's one of the great exceptions—when you find born leaders so sold out to God that they realize that they owe all of their success to God, not to themselves. When you find a leader like this you have found your next small group coordinator, director, or even pastor. This person is best used developing leaders. But be careful, because this same person without humility and submission to God will create more problems than he or she will solve.

The Lifetime Church Ministry Leader

Many people who have been ministry leaders their entire lives in one church or another sometimes want everything their way instead of following your process. Every small group leader needs to be able to follow the leadership to be a part of the ministry. In a thriving church everyone is under the authority of someone else.

That is true for the leadership of small groups. They are under your authority or someone to whom you delegate the authority. Otherwise the process falls apart. We've seen this happen many times, especially in mainline churches where biblical authority is usually absent. You must have a plan and carry it out as the leader of the ministry, and anyone who challenges that authority should not be in leadership.

We know these are strong words, but just a few people with a different vision can do a huge amount of damage in a very short time. Sometimes your small group system may have to get smaller to get healthier. Tough choices, of course, but what is more important, a few people's feelings or the health of the entire ministry? At some point you may have to ask yourself, "Do I work for God or a few disgruntled people?"

The Perfect Life Person

The lack of humility it takes to believe one is perfect is a recipe for failure as a leader. You don't need a Savior if you think you're perfect. You'll find people who truly believe they have all the answers. Instead of persons who think they have all the answers, look for people who are trying every day to become more like Christ and look to God for forgiveness when they fall short. These folks aren't perfect, and they know it. These are the people you want to lead your small groups, because they're humble.

The Finished Race Person

This person thinks they have already made it. If persons think they've made it they are in no way prepared to lead anyone. This person is really kind of a combination of all the rest all wrapped up in one, which is a recipe for disaster. Your small groups are in far better hands with leaders who know they have a long way to go and are humbly willing to share their successes and failures with others in their groups.

Moving On

All the people we talked about previously who don't make the best leaders are the very people everyone thinks should lead because they're viewed as more spiritual. The people who make the best small group leaders look at the knowledge other people have and that makes them feel unworthy. Don't look at people's knowledge; look at their heart! God can work with a person with a good heart regardless of his or her knowledge. You want leaders who are humble enough to know they need God's help and will ask for it.

Coaching Time

- Be careful with the people who come running up to you telling you what great leaders they will be. These people tend to make it all about themselves.
- Did anyone come to mind as you read through the types of people to avoid in leadership or in a small group? If so, how are you going to handle them?
- If you already have small groups in place, do any of your leaders fit any of the personalities listed in this chapter? If so, what can you do about it?

CHAPTER SEVEN

TRAINING FUTURE LEADERS: PART ONE

Step Eight: Train Your Leadership

Okay, so you have collected a group of leaders. Step eight is to train those leaders. These two chapters contain a Leader's Training Manual that you can use in your training. This manual addresses every single issue we have ever faced doing small groups. It needs to be discussed in actual training sessions as well as taken home by everyone in the small group so that they can refer back to it when they need help with a specific problem. We suggest that you give this book to each of your small group leaders so they can have these two chapters.

What Is a Healthy Small Group?

You can't expect people to lead something they can't define. So in a nutshell, here is the definition of the kind of healthy small group that changes lives.

A healthy small group is:

- A community of ten to fifteen people coming together weekly or biweekly to help one another grow closer to God.
- A diverse collection of very different individuals with different backgrounds, incomes, levels of faith, and varying views of people and the world who have some form of affinity.

- A place where people can come as they are and know they are accepted with all their faults and failings.
- Always open to new people. Nothing will kill a small group ministry faster than unwelcoming, closed groups, because it creates a social club for Christians where no new Christian or non-Christian will ever feel welcome.
- A safe place. For people to really open up and begin to share life together, they must know that what they talk about stays in the group.
- Built on *authentic* relationships. Nothing significant ever happens in a small group without first building up loving and trusting relationships. The very success of this ministry is driven by relationships.
- Fun. If the group isn't fun it won't last. Bible studies are designed to be educational, not fun. People will not come back week after week for just a Bible study.
- A group that multiplies. Keep a group together for too long, and it will become unhealthy. Are there exceptions? Not many! New people bring new lifeblood to a group. Healthy small groups should be expected to multiply at least by the end of the first year. For strong and gifted leaders, that time should be cut in half.
- A producer of leaders and servants. Existing small groups are the training ground for future leaders and the volunteers needed to keep the church growing. Later we will talk about the importance of each small group leader having one or two leaders in training.

It's All about Balance

For a small group to be able to be a life-changing force, it must have the right balance in three main areas—shepherding, teaching, and fellowship. Small groups that focus primarily on just one or two of these usually fail.

Let's talk about balance and how to achieve it and what the consequences are when it doesn't happen. We will do this by looking at the three keys to a healthy small group and showing how even good things without balance will contribute to unhealthy groups.

The Shepherding Small Group

This small group focuses all its energy on meeting the personal needs of the people. Every group should be caring and loving, but these groups often become therapy sessions for the problem of the week. This doesn't mean that the group shouldn't care about people's struggles. It does mean, however, that if the group is about nothing but people complaining week after week, it will become so negative that people won't come back because it's basic human nature for people to be drawn to a positive message.

The question we get is, "When is it appropriate to deal with people's struggles?" When someone in the group has been an active part of the group, has given of themselves to others, and is seen as a positive influence in the group and now needs the group to rally around him or her for some reason, by all means skip the curriculum and pour your hearts out on that person. When people like this are in need the group should be there for them, because they have been there for the group! But such response can't be a recurring event or the group will die.

The Teaching Small Group

This group focuses completely on the Bible and knowledge. It is usually led by someone who thinks he or she is the Bible champion of the free world and won't quit until every person in the group has reached his or her level. The problem is that these types of people tend to set themselves up as the standard for others to aspire to. Most people go to a small group because they are looking for a place where they can feel like they belong. Of course there should be a teaching aspect to every group, but it will not be successful if that's the only focus. Life change happens through the relationships that are built in the group, and those kinds of relationships suffer when the group becomes completely about knowledge. These groups often become unhealthy because of the arrogance of the leader. You must not allow knowledge to replace love in your groups.

The Fellowship Small Group

This group loves fellowship. They eat together, laugh together, do game nights at meetings, go out together during the week, and just enjoy their time talking and socializing at the group. All of these things are awesome and necessary. However, if you're not careful you will have a bunch of groups that never get around to anything meaningful or life-changing. This was the biggest problem I (Bill) faced with my first attempt at small groups. What I found was that groups that focus on fellowship never multiply. So I had to start over.

These groups always start off great because people are looking for this kind of fellowship. But small groups are also about life-change, and if lives aren't changed people eventually leave. God must be a part of every group every time it meets. In a purely social setting that doesn't happen.

The Right Balance

Healthy small groups offer a healthy balance. First, they want to be a group like the shepherding group where people reach out and help one another. Second, they want to be a group that looks at the Word of God to guide them to real and permanent life-change. Third, they want to have fun and build authentic relationships that extend outside the walls of the church and even the homes in which they are meeting. We strongly urge you to make sure all small groups have shepherding, teaching, and fellowship but that the overarching goal is a life-change in the individuals in the group.

What Is the Goal of a Small Group?

The primary goal of every group is to produce changed lives. Small groups exist so people will have a place to fellowship and grow closer to God by sharing life together through a combination of fun, fellowship, Bible study, and prayer.

- Small groups exist to relationally connect the church body. This connection is vital to the future and the continued growth of any church. Some people think small groups help the church grow. Not so. They help the growing church *retain* those who are coming to worship. However, your church won't continue to grow past its ability to stay connected and retain those already worshiping.

- Small groups are a place to train future leaders. It is the job of every small group leader to reproduce their leadership in others from their group. Every small group leader should have one or two leaders in training within the first month or two. Most small group systems fail because they do not understand this point.

- Small groups are a place to recruit servants. Each small group leader should have a goal of 100 percent participation in a church ministry by its attendees. Nothing advances the life-change process more than serving in a ministry at the church. God is a proactive God and wants our participation in advancing the Kingdom. Small groups are a place to talk about and teach the concepts of service as well as help each person find a place to serve.

- Small groups are a place to begin teaching biblical principles. What makes small groups unique is that these principles are taught in the privacy of a home with a group of people who already love one another. These strong relationships create an atmosphere of trust and confidentiality where real life-change can happen. People want to talk about the tough issues of life, but they need a safe place to discuss them. The best teaching in small groups comes from shared experiences. Nothing is more powerful than someone telling a group of people what God has done in their lives. In the privacy of a home, that story often includes incredible honesty of past sins and struggles.

- Small groups are expected to be confidential. The single most important rule at any small group is, "What's said in the group stays in the group." People need to know that when they share their most intimate and private experiences, they never leave the room. Every group needs to start off the first meeting with this rule and remind the people about the rule every time a new person comes to the group. When privacy dies, so does your group. The rule is so important that breaking that trust is grounds for removing someone from the group or leadership.

When small groups achieve these goals you have created a life-changing machine in your church.

Why Do People Need to Be in a Small Group?

God didn't intend for us to go it alone. We were created for fellowship. God said, "It is not good for the man to be alone."[1] The Bible constantly uses terms like put together, joined together, built together, members together, heirs together, fitted together, and held together. Together, together, together.[2]

How Do You Get People to Join Your Small Groups?

- First and foremost *pray.* Ministry leaders need to pray for the ministry, its leaders, and their own leadership. Small group leaders must pray for their group, for the individuals who are struggling in the group, for God to help them become the best leaders they can be, and for God to show them what the needs of their people are and how they can serve them. Of course, they will also pray before and after each group meeting, and most groups share prayer requests at some point in the meeting.
- Have events such as a small group rally. If you plan well more people will join your ministry in one day than the other 364 days together. If one rally a year is working well, try two a year. BAF does two every year. We will talk in depth about this rally later.
- Insert a small group sign-up form in the regular weekly bulletin. Make sure it says what a small group is and why people should join one. They can be dropped in the offering, or you can have a place to drop them as people leave.
- Hand the inserts out as people enter the worship area. Most churches have some high-travel area where volunteers can hand out information on small groups.
- Have a small group page on your Web site. Create a sign-up form on that page that is automatically forwarded to the ministry leader in charge of making personal contacts.
- Set up a small group information table in a central place. Have small group leaders in place who can discuss the min-

istry with those interested. Make sure if someone wants to join a group they can give him or her information right then and there.

- Leaders and attendees need to personally invite people to their groups. Let your people know that these groups are open to anyone. Don't even require that they attend your church to be a part of a group. If someone's life can be changed by your group, invite them!

- When people indicate an interest in small groups, send their names to the office of the pastor of small groups. Each name is then sent out to a small group coordinator. Each coordinator is required to maintain regular contact with the pastor's office so the particular needs of the group are known. This allows the pastor's office to know whose groups need people. A record of each name and which coordinator it was sent to is kept in the office of the small group pastor for accountability.

- Names are then sent to an appropriate small group by the coordinator and a record of which group the name was sent to is logged. Prior to sending the names out, the coordinator is required to make a courtesy call to these persons letting them know they are in the system and should be receiving a call from a leader soon. Coordinators are required to give the person their phone number so they can call if they have not received a call from a leader in a timely manner. These calls are very important because they set the tone of the ministry. They must be done in an inviting way that leaves people excited about the upcoming call from a leader.

- After receiving the contact information each small group leader is required to make at least three calls to the homes of the people who are looking for a group. Ask each leader to try more than one type of contact if that information is available (e-mail, cell phone, home phone, work phone, etc.). Each small group leader should be required to keep a log of the times and dates of those contacts for accountability reasons. If all of these procedures are followed there is always a way to see where the system failed if someone who filled out the information wasn't called. In 95 percent of the cases, when someone is upset because no one has called, you will be able to track that back to a leader who has left multiple messages on multiple numbers. This system will protect the integrity of the ministry and its leaders. It is primarily the role of coordinators to make sure that each part of this system operates in the way it is designed.

For all of these ideas to work the lead pastor must regularly recast the vision for small groups. Your small group ministry must be kept in the hearts and minds of the people in the church, and they must be reminded regularly why they need to join a group.

Coaching Corner

- If you already have a small group system, how balanced is it?
- If you don't have one keep in mind the need for overall balance.
- Does your plan for getting people into small groups have a system of accountability set up in it?
- In reading this chapter did you understand that successfully getting people to join small groups requires the use of many different methods?
- Do you realize that getting people into small groups is an ongoing process that never ends?

Notes

1. Genesis 2:18.
2. Rick Warren in *The Purpose Driven Life* (Grand Rapids: Zondervan, 2002) references these "togethers" on page 130.

CHAPTER EIGHT

TRAINING FUTURE LEADERS: PART TWO

Step Eight: Train Your Leadership

Any time you bring together a group of people from different backgrounds and experiences you will have personality issues. If you aren't dealing with problems in your small groups, it's because you haven't created a safe, life-changing place for people to talk about their problems. Often these problems emerge the third or fourth month in the life of a group because by then the group has reached the point of intimacy and trust. When that happens, problems usually arise. Your leaders must be equipped to deal with them.

Problems and Solutions

This chapter discusses all of the potential personality issues we've dealt with over the years. It's important to know that these examples come from many different small groups, so don't expect to find all of the issues discussed below in one small group. Knowing about these issues and how to handle them is critical to the success of a small group. One of the greatest failures of small group pastors and lay leaders is sending new small group leaders out unprepared for the situations they may face in their homes.

One of the toughest issues any small group leader will ever

face is critical people. People who want to make the small group a place to criticize either the church, its leadership, or other people. Jesus gave us the answer on how to deal with these situations, so let's look at his teaching and then apply it to some situations that small group leaders may face.

The Importance of Using Mathew 18:15-17

Matthew 18:15-17 is scripture that every small group leader should memorize. So, let's walk through it step by step and learn what Jesus taught about how to deal with these kinds of issues and why, as a leader, when you put it into practice you can save yourself a lot of heartache.

- Step One: "If another believer sins against you, go privately and point out the offense. If the other person listens and confesses it, you have won that person back."
- Step Two: "But if you are unsuccessful, take one or two others with you and go back again, so that everything you say may be confirmed by two or three witnesses."
- Step Three: "If the person still refuses to listen, take your case to the church."
- Step Four: "Then if he or she won't accept the church's decision, treat that person as a pagan or a corrupt tax collector."

We can't underestimate the importance of this text for dealing with critical people. Following Jesus' example ensures that you and your group do not become deeply embroiled in personality issues.

Let's look at some situations that small group leaders may face and how to apply Matthew 18 to them.

Criticism of the Church, Its Leadership, or Other Christians

When someone tries to use a small group to attack the church or its leadership each leader must be ready to deal with it before it gets out of hand. Below are examples of how to use Matthew 18:15-17 to deal with these situations without the entire group paying the price.

When someone tries to attack the church, leaders need to be prepared to say the following: "I appreciate that you may have a problem or conflict with the church. However, as the small group leader I want you to know that I completely support the vision and pastors of our church and our group just isn't a place to discuss this kind of thing.

"If you have a problem with church leadership, I want to encourage you to go talk to someone at the church and share your concerns. I'm sure a church leader would be happy to talk to you about this. Matthew 18:15-17 doesn't allow me to discuss this with you (or in the group) before you address this issue biblically with the person with whom you have this problem."

If an individual has a problem with a specific pastor or staff member, you should also be prepared to invoke Matthew 18:15-17 by asking the question, "Have you talked to him or her about this issue?" This should be followed up with the statement, "I would love to talk to you about this, but Matthew 18:15 says you are to talk to that person first before I can even discuss it with you." In most cases that will be the end of the issue because most people don't have a deep enough conviction on these issues to actually confront the person. And if they do it will be done in the way Jesus tells us to do it.

Criticism of Other People in the Church or Small Group

If someone wants to use the group to criticize other people you must not allow it. Let everyone know that the steps outlined in Matthew 18 for attack of the church and its leadership apply here as well.

Here's where it can get tough. When someone comes to you and wants you to listen to his or her criticisms, it's human nature to want to step in and try to help fix the situation. Jesus gives an outline for dealing with this, and you will regret it every time you don't follow it.

The following is a list of things that can happen when you don't follow Matthew 18 when dealing with people who want to criticize or attack others. If you are a small group pastor, lay leader, coordinator, or group leader, read this carefully and it will save you a lot of pain.

- If you allow yourself to get involved even just a little bit, you will be completely involved before you know it.
- You will find yourself taking a side without having all the facts. Most of the time you won't realize you didn't get the entire story until it's too late. No matter what you feel the true story is, there are *always* two sides, and the truth almost always lies somewhere between the two.
- You may find yourself giving advice on issues you really know nothing about. Even worse, you may give bad advice thinking you did the right thing only to find out how much damage was done with your advice.
- You will set a precedent to the rest of the group that you are their counselor and problem-fixer—something you will live to regret.
- The problem will grow and work its way into the rest of the group because the same person talking to you about this is talking to others in the small group also. If you apply Matthew 18 it usually stops the criticism in its tracks.

And the worst consequences to not following Jesus are these:

- It will turn out horribly.
- Someone will hate you.
- After it's over and the damage is done, you'll remember that God gave you all the directions you needed and you didn't listen.

Dealing with Individuals Who Want to Make the Group All about Them

Persons who want to make themselves the center of attention seem to turn up in most groups. A number of people fall into this category, and each of them presents a unique problem for the small group leader. Before you read this section remember our desire is to help people change and to love all of God's people. However, if you don't find ways to handle these kinds of extreme personalities, everyone else will leave your group. You may have people in your group who struggle with some of these issues and aren't really causing much of a problem. We're not writing about them. The following examples are the extreme problem-causers.

The single person who seems to always be dating the wrong people. People who constantly make bad choices also aren't very good at looking inward to see what part of their relationship failures are their fault. So they use the group as a sounding board for the newest relationship issue of the day. These people always have a new issue because they are continually making bad choices in their dating lives. This personality type is usually the one who thinks everything bad that has ever happened in his or her life is somebody else's fault. One person making the group his or her personal counseling session week after week will drive people to another group.

Don't make the mistake, however, of confusing the selfish people who care about no one but themselves with the people who are really trying to change their lives and need help to learn how to make better choices in the people they date. One is a person who doesn't care about anyone else, and the other is a person seeking the guidance and support needed to learn to grow closer to God. Experienced leaders learn to recognize the difference and know how to handle these issues. That's why your best leaders usually come from existing groups where they learn how to handle these situations before they become leaders. Relational issues are much more prevalent in singles groups, so spend significantly more time preparing your singles leaders for these kinds of issues. I (John) am now meeting with my singles small group leaders every six to eight weeks. This kind of ongoing training is possible with singles because, in most cases, they have the time and, frankly, it's necessary in order to keep the ministry healthy.

The person who is very lonely or completely alone. These people are usually nice people, but their small group often becomes the only thing in their lives. These people will overwhelm the group with stories of how bad their lives are. Don't embarrass them publicly, but privately take the time to help them grow. Find a way to help these people see a future with hope by spending some personal time talking about some of their issues. People are drawn to a positive message and will reject a group that is driven by negativity.

The people who just like to hear themselves talk. This person will overwhelm anyone who wants to talk and always has to top every story with one of their own that is better. If you're not careful this person will be the only one talking every week. People will

65

grow weary of it and leave. Every group seems to have one of these. If you don't help this person grow he or she will destroy your group then move on to another one and begin breaking it down too! When this happens just say, "Mary, there are a lot of people here tonight who haven't yet been heard from. Surely you want to hear what they have to share. So let's give them a chance to speak for the rest of the meeting."

The "it's all about me" person. This person always shows up late and without regard for the rest of the people in the group, walks around the house eating and talking on a cell phone while the others are in their study and discussion time. This kind of behavior requires a sufficiently large amount of arrogance and selfishness, and it will hurt the others' ability to learn and grow. These persons will never change until someone tells them they need to. Confrontation is a part of leadership. Again this will best be done outside of the group.

The parents that allow their kids to run wild through the group. Your groups with children should have some type of child-care set up. If the group continues to be interrupted then the system in place is not working. The entire group should not have to suffer because one parent can't control his or her children. Childcare issues are always difficult. But you must find a solution because people will just quit coming. Parents should understand that when a child interrupts the group, it's their responsibility to get up and take the child to another room so the rest of the group can continue. This is a boundary; set it and stick to it for the sake of the rest of the group. We will discuss childcare issues in an upcoming chapter.

The person who will stay around for hours after everyone else leaves without regard for your time. Have a starting and ending time for the group. Hold your ground, and tell everyone from day one that you need them to honor this. If you don't start this from day one it will come back to bite you. If an ending time is not important that's fine, but if you want people to leave in a timely manner you need to set that boundary from the very beginning. Explain to them the value of your time and why you need them to respect this boundary.

The person who thinks he or she knows more than the leader. This person will make you mad if you're not careful. These people are usually very strong willed and won't go easily. They will also be the people who come to you to tell you what great leaders they would be. You will most likely have to confront this person, and it usually will not turn out well. Small group leaders need to contact their ministry leader and discuss this person with him or her. The ministry leader needs to know about this, because you can rest assured this person is going to gripe and complain to anyone who will listen. If a person doesn't respond well to the confrontation he or she will leave and go do the same thing at another group, so make sure a real problem person is reported to the ministry leadership.

As you read about these people please remember that God loves them and so should we. However, if these issues are not addressed and solved, the selfish or even legitimate needs of one person will destroy the needs of the rest of the group.

You will find some of these people in your groups and that's fine because a small group that only deals with the good stuff and never takes on any tough issues will eventually fall apart because nothing real is happening. Sharing life together means just that— sharing the good and the bad of life so everyone can grow together. If you're sharing the bad too you will have people who require extra effort. One of the toughest things in leadership is knowing when to pour your heart into someone and when to let that person move on. Effective leaders learn to trust their instinct.

The key to dealing with personality issues: "Are the persons involved giving something to the group or are they there to see what they can get from the group?"

The key to understanding when to confront these issues is to look at the person's history and make a judgment as to his or her involvement in the group and desire to serve others. This is one of the toughest things a leader will face because you will be afraid others in the group will think you have been too harsh. Of course you want people to come to your group with the tough issues they really want to talk about because that is what the group is for. The difference we're talking about is when the same person has the same problems week after week and wants to make the group completely about him or her all the time. That person will ruin the group for everyone else.

Then there's the person who really is trying to change his or her life and is struggling with something. In that situation don't be afraid to throw out the planned lesson and talk about something going on in someone's life. In fact, those can be some of the best meetings you'll ever have because you're dealing with real-life issues. However, remember that as good as those times were, you have to be careful or something positive will end up negative if every time you meet you are dealing with the same person and the same issues. Too much of a good thing can become excessive. Meet people's needs as needed; just don't continue to make every single meeting about the need of the week. Your group will become a counseling session each week if you do, and you don't want that to happen. Ask God to teach you discernment so you can know when something is worthy of the group's time.

Answering Tough Questions

One of the greatest fears any potential leader has is being asked biblical questions they can't answer. Here are some key things to remember about tough questions.

- No one has all the answers. If we were to wait until we had leaders with all the answers, there would be no small group ministry.
- You're going to give the wrong answer at some point thinking you are right. Be humble and admit you made a mistake and people will be drawn to your humility and honesty. Move past your mistakes by admitting to them.
- Saying "I don't know" is okay. Just follow it up with "But I'll do my best to find out."
- Don't give an answer if you don't know the answer, especially when it comes to the Bible. Giving the wrong answer is worse than saying "I don't know." Be humble enough to just say you don't know.
- When you get a tough question and don't know the answer, research it yourself first and see if you can find the answer.

This process will grow you as a leader. If you are struggling then get in touch with your small group pastor or coordinator and discuss the issues with him or her. When you come up with the answer make sure you discuss it in the group. Don't just go to the person who asked it; use your group time to discuss it so everyone can grow from the exercise. Talk with the group about the process of finding the answer.

Dealing with Disagreements in the Group

When you bring a group of diverse people together you will have some disagreements from time to time. Any disagreement can turn out fine if it is handled right from the beginning. Below are some examples of these kinds of situations and how best to handle them.

Disagreements about Biblical Issues

The time will come when you have a heated discussion about some biblical principle. People's feelings about biblical issues usually stem from some past life or church experience, which could either have been positive or damaging. It is important to try to understand where someone has come from and why he or she feels that way about a particular issue in the Bible. This may be one of those times when you have to say, "Let's get back to this next week," so that you can be better prepared and know exactly what the Bible says about this particular issue. Tell everyone in the room that you will find out all the information on this subject and be ready to talk about it at the next meeting. Don't let a biblical disagreement issue get out of hand and turn ugly. It can happen before you know it, because when someone takes a stand on an issue like this it's very hard to back off and accept that he or she may be wrong. If possible take time to relax and move on until the next meeting when you're ready to address the issue.

Explain to your people that men and women, who have dedicated their entire lives to studying the Bible, disagree on many translation issues in the Bible. With some translation disagreements you have to just agree to disagree.

A great way to move past a theological disagreement is to focus the group on what we all can agree on as opposed to what we don't agree about. What we all agree on is that Jesus is the Son of God and he came to die for our sins. The last thing we would say is, The main message of the Bible doesn't change because we can't agree on every translation issue. Just say, "Let's get back to the basics that all Christians from all denominations can agree on, and that is Jesus."

Sounds easy, doesn't it! Well, sometimes it is and sometimes it isn't, but if agreeing to disagree is what it takes then do it. We're clearly not saying you should allow heresy in your groups for the sake of unity. There is a difference between heresy and translation disagreements. Heresy will break and separate the group, so it must not be allowed. You will learn to know the difference, but if you're not sure that's when you need to ask for help so the problem can be solved and the group can move forward.

The key here is never to let the Bible be a stumbling block to a healthy group. God did not create the Bible to separate us. Don't allow this to happen in your group. Lean on your leadership here to help you get through this kind of tough and emotional issue.

Disagreements about What the Small Group Should Be

What the small group is going to be like should be decided by the small group leader prior to inviting anyone into the group. Each group should be a reflection of the leader who has been called by God to lead that group. But sometimes people may not be happy until they change the group to be exactly what they want it to be. Certainly what people want and think is important, but make sure that you don't ever let someone take your group hostage. Instead of changing the group each time someone doesn't like the way it's being run, encourage that person to try some other group.

Dealing with Tough Family Problems and Issues

Family issues always wiggle their way into groups. As a church interested in bringing people to Christ, you are always welcoming people into your church who often know little or nothing about Christ. These folk arrive with all the problems associated with lives separated from God. Your small group may be the only healthy family experience they have. Deal with these issues with love and care, but be very careful not to become a family counselor.

Many family issues are so severe that they require professional counseling. Tread lightly here because it's human nature to want to help fix these problems. We suggest that you form an alliance with a nonprofit family Christian counseling service and encourage your small group leaders to refer people to professionals when the issues are deep and painful. The worst thing you can do is give bad advice that could affect someone's life. These issues will also completely overwhelm your group, and you will find yourself knee-deep in counseling week after week.

Remember, the small group is a place of caring and love, and as you grow in your leadership you will begin to recognize the difference in reaching out to those in the group and becoming a counselor. The group's job is to support these families as they go through professional counseling, not to become a counseling session. If you have a situation like this and are not sure how to handle it, then ask for help.

Keeping the Group Together

Once there has been an argument in your group, and there will be, how do you keep the group together? Conflict in the group is often the opening for major growth of the group, but it must be resolved in the group. If there is a conflict in the group the worst possible thing you can do is hope it will go away. It never does. Ignoring it will destroy the group. So you must deal with it.

When tempers are high it is not the best time to try to settle an issue. Let everyone calm down, and tell the group that this will be talked about next week. But do not sweep it under the rug.

Before the next meeting spend time talking with each party privately to find out where the anger came from. When someone attacks another person it usually has less to do with what happened in the small group and more to do with what is going on in that person's life. Get the parties together if possible, away from the group, and let there be some healing before it is talked about at the next meeting. The people involved may still not agree on the issue, but the group needs to see them agree to disagree and still be friends.

Having said that, there may be times when agreeing to disagree just won't work. In this situation find out what God's Word says about the issue and take a stand on what is right regardless of the outcome. If a person's stance goes against the Word of God he or she will have to be shown the truth in love regardless of how it's received.

Leaders can't be prepared to deal with these kinds of issues if they themselves are not spending time in the Word and in prayer. Too many leaders get in trouble by not praying and asking God for guidance. They tend to try to fix things on their own. Both of us know from experience that you just must not leave God out of the equation. Make sure you have prayed through the situation and have a plan to get things back on track.

Moving On

The best advice we can give you on how to deal with each of these situations is to *lead*. Begin by talking to your group about healthy boundaries in their lives. Lead by example by having healthy boundaries in your life. From day one, talk about the group and what it is and what it's not. Make sure people know that if they are coming to the group with the attitude of "what can the group do for me," they are there for the wrong reason. Every person should be there to see what they can give to the group. The people in your group need to know that every person has a unique gift that God wants to use to minister to someone else (Romans 12). Start day one with the statement, "It's not about you; it's about the community and what you can do for it." When everyone in the group truly begins to understand this concept then everyone will be a shepherd and also be shepherded. This is the basis for a healthy small group.

Coaching Time

- What system do you have in place for small group leaders to turn to when they need help with an issue?

- How do you feel about using Matthew 18 for all of the above situations?
- Have you prepared your leaders to deal with problem people in small groups?
- Do your leaders understand why problem people must be dealt with? If not, they won't do it because it's easier to avoid a confrontation.

CHAPTER NINE

THE SMALL GROUP LEADER'S ROLE

Step Nine: Create Ownership

The role of a small group leader is to create a safe, comfortable, and loving environment where people can change their lives and grow in their faith as they share life together. In order for that to happen small groups must be healthy. The way to keep unhealthy small groups out of your church is to have a solid model that is designed to create life-change, not dissension, and not even Bible study. You accomplish such a model not by just hoping and praying that your groups will end up healthy, but by creating a healthy model from day one. The key to this health is to create a place where everyone who attends a group feels ownership of the group—not that they are just attending, but that it is their group. Nothing solid will really happen in your small group system until the small group leaders make sure ownership happens.

From day one work toward everyone having a responsibility within the group.

Create Ownership and Have a Plan

Ownership happens when every person in the group is involved in some part of the group. If the people coming to the group simply show up and get fed, the group will never be anything more than a place where people come to see what the group can do for them. To change that attitude you need to create an atmosphere where people are coming to see what they can do for the group. You do this by making sure every person has a role in making the group work. When everyone is using their gifts the group is stronger.

Creating ownership achieves three goals. First, no one burns out; second, you raise up future leaders; and third, the rest of the group takes ownership. Here are some examples of how you assist in the group taking ownership as well as birthing new leaders.

> *Ownership happens when every person in the group is involved in some part of the group.*

In order for ownership to occur, consider at least the following areas of service:

- The person who has the personality to deal with people. This person can be the contact person who calls and invites people to the group and/or e-mails and reminds people that the group is coming up and that he or she is looking forward to seeing them.
- The person or persons who are gifted in scheduling. This person is also responsible for making sure everyone in the group is taking a turn at bringing food.
- Someone who can handle special events. He or she can plan events that happen outside the regular weekly meeting.
- The person drawn to prayer. He or she can oversee making sure each prayer request is covered, as well as plan to have a night when the group goes back through the old prayer requests to see what God has been doing with them.
- The hospitality person who meets and greets each week.
- The people who like to help clean up after the group.
- Move the group to different homes so the same person doesn't always have to get his or her place ready.

Always be looking for your next leader to take your place. You want this person, in time, to either be able to lead the group or move on to form another group. Give this person a growing responsibility in the leading of your small group.

> *If you need to, create positions that aren't really that necessary if they will get someone personally involved.*

Here's the key: when every person attending the group begins to call it "my group" instead of "the group," you're on the right track.

Making sure everyone in the group is involved is not only healthy for the group but it is also healthy for the leaders. When leaders try to do everything for the group they end up burning out. Watch for burned-out leaders, because they usually won't admit they're burned out until they have spent six months just going through the motions.

Leading an Actual Small Group Meeting

Leading a small group for the first time can be a daunting experience. Often the small group leaders are full of questions, especially if they have never been in a small group. Many of your leaders will come from other small groups, but many come from the vision-casting of your pastor during worship. Many will open up their homes having never even attended a small group of any kind. Often these are some of the best leaders because they are simply being obedient to God's call.

So let's walk through what a typical two-hour small group might look like and talk about some options. We're going to use the actual model used at Bay Area Fellowship. You will want to tailor your small group to fit your setting. We just make one word of caution: Whatever model you choose to put into effect, make sure it stresses

- leadership development
- multiplication of groups and leaders

- lead pastor support
- and life-change

If you have these four elements in place your model should work.

The Beginning

Typically you will start your group with a time of fellowship. Have some food available. Some groups do full-blown meals, and others do light snacks and drinks. Find out which option your people prefer and make sure they join in by bringing something. Most groups assign someone to handle the food issues, and that person schedules different people to bring food at different times. This fellowship time is for people to get to know one another or talk about what is going on in their lives. This is one of the most important parts of the group because it's relationship building. This time usually runs from 30 to 45 minutes. If you skip this part of the group you will not have a group for long. The health of the group comes from the quality of the relationships. But be careful to manage this time or you will find yourself doing nothing but fellowship.

The Teaching and Application

After the fellowship, call everyone to the central meeting area to begin the study part of the group. Begin with a prayer, then begin your study and make sure that you don't make this time a traditional Bible study. Of course, you are using the Word of God as the teaching guide, but make the lesson practical, so that the group learns through shared experiences and life application of God's Word.

Good leaders always make sure that people are talking among themselves and not only to the leader. Your small group will blossom when everyone is participating in the discussions. Be patient with those who are not ready and let them just listen until they are ready to participate in the discussions.

Don't ever let anyone tell you that sharing life experiences and teaching the Bible through life application is not discipleship. One of the best ways for someone to see God's love is through the love of Christians representing Christ pouring their hearts out on another person.

Keep the Group Balanced

A small group leader should make sure the group has a balance of all the important elements that ensure the group's health. Below is a list of the things that make for balance.

- **Fun.** Every small group leader must create an atmosphere of fun so that people will be committed to coming back. People will not come back week after week to a boring group. Laughter and fun will bring them back.
- **Relationships.** Relationships are the key to making sure groups are fun and meaningful. The small group leader's role is to create an atmosphere of fun so relationships will happen.
- **A well-run group.** Many small groups fail because of lazy leaders. They don't call people, e-mail people, or do anything more than open their homes a couple of times a month. The small group leader's role is to make sure all the necessary elements are taken care of.
- **A feeling of love and acceptance.** Small group leaders need to make sure that every person that comes to the group, either existing or new, feels loved and accepted.
- **Preparation.** One of our biggest pet peeves is leaders that regularly come to their group unprepared to lead. They have not gone over the material and many times never get to anything other than the fellowship aspect of the group. I (John) have had to tell leaders that if they aren't willing to get prepared to lead their group, they're doing a disservice to God and the ministry. In several cases, I (Bill) had to remove a small group leader because it was obvious from the small group experience that he had a habit of not doing any preparation.
- **Raising up new leaders.** Small group leaders should know by now that one of the most important roles they have is to reproduce their leadership in others and prepare them for multiplication. This is *the* most important role they have. See chapter 4 for more on raising up new leaders.

Moving On

The role of the small group leader is the heart of any solid small group system. No amount of time and energy is too much to spend on raising up and equipping these leaders to lead their group. They grow and so does the community factor of your church.

Coaching Time

- Using the list we have provided, make a list of all of the possible responsibilities for a small group.
- Do you have a plan for raising up new leaders? This is the toughest issue you will face, and it will not happen on its own.
- Is the role of small group leaders clearly defined? If not, leaders will define it for you, which is not what you want to happen.

CHAPTER TEN

FILLING UP YOUR SMALL GROUPS

Step Ten: Fill Your Small Groups

L et's assume that your leaders are chosen and trained. Now we can begin discussing the nuts and bolts of how to start, fill, run, manage, and grow a small group ministry.

The Small Group Rally

Let's begin with the things you need to do to get your small groups filled up. Many ways exist to get a new or stagnant small group ministry up and running, but in our experience nothing works as well as a small group rally. BAF does at least two small group rallies a year because they are so successful. BAF does many things throughout the year to get people into their groups and we'll talk about them as we go, but more people join their smalll group ministry in the two days of the rallies than the rest of the year put together.

A smalll group rally is like a rallying point where you bring together a large group of people who are looking to join a small group. To do a small group rally you need a space large enough to accommodate the number of people you expect to attend. You will need to set up a space for new leaders starting for the first time, and for groups that need to get jump-started. This space consists of no more than a couple of chairs and a table. Each leader prepares a handout with all his or her contact information, dates and times of the group, as well as directions to the home where the group will be held. Leaders also have an information card available for interested people to fill out so the leaders can call them before the first meeting and encourage them to attend. Set up some snacks and drinks, and play music in the background.

The idea is to create a fun and exciting atmosphere where people can walk around and meet different leaders and find a group they feel fits them. What makes the rally work so well is that each new person attending can meet multiple leaders and choose one with whom he or she connects. Another key to the success of the rally is that it's full of people and there is real energy in the room and people are drawn to it.

A rally usually lasts a couple of hours, and people will come and go throughout that time. Make sure you have childcare available and let everyone know you're providing it.

Be ready for the people who were not able to find a group that fits them. Have some of your more experienced leaders move around the room with clipboards taking information from the people who still want a group but haven't found one so that they can be placed in other groups later. Use your most experienced people so they can answer all the questions people might have. Require your smalll group coordinators to attend all rallies. They are there to help anyone with any problems. Since it's not possible to always have a group for everyone, the coordinators make sure every person finds a group, even if they don't find a group at the rally.

Getting People to Attend the Rally

Here is where we go back to the part about making sure you have completed step one, which was to make sure your lead pastor and official body are all on board with the concept of small groups. You need your lead pastor to be the vision-caster for the ministry and for the rally and for why the people need to join a small group.

Prior to the rally your lead pastor needs to do a two- to three-week preaching series on fellowship and relationships. The whole idea is to convince people that they need to attend the rally and join a small group. How do you sell them on this? Teach what God says about making this walk together and not alone.

Using a Sermon Series to Fill Up Small Groups

Nowhere in the Bible does it say anything about making your walk with God alone. Sure, God sent some people out to the desert in order to grow them and prepare them for the task ahead, but God never left them out there because God didn't create us to be alone. Rick Warren puts it best in his book *The Purpose-Driven Life* where he says,

> The Bible knows nothing of solitary saints or spiritual hermits isolated from other believers and deprived of fellowship. The Bible says we are put together, joined together, built together, members together, heirs together, fitted together, and held together and will be caught up together. You're not on your own anymore.[1]

Scripture is clear that God wants us to love him first and each other second, and that is the basis for why each person in your church needs to be in a small group.

The following is an example of a sermon series designed to prepare your people for the small group rally.

The basis of the message might be "Not Trying to Go It Alone," and the scripture texts might include some of the following:

> The LORD God said, "It is not good for the man to be alone." (Genesis 2:18 NIV)

> Share each other's burdens, and in this way obey the law of Christ. (Galatians 6:2 NLT)

> I mean that I want us to help each other with the faith we have. Your faith will help me, and my faith will help you. (Romans 1:12 NCV)

> In this way we are like the various parts of a human body. Each part gets its meaning from the body as a whole, not the other way around. The body we're

talking about is Christ's body of chosen people. Each of us finds our meaning and function as a part of his body. But as a chopped-off finger or cut-off toe we wouldn't amount to much, would we? (Romans 12:4-5 The Message)

Now you are no longer strangers to God and foreigners to heaven, but you are members of God's very own family, citizens of God's country and you belong in God's household with every other Christian. (Ephesians 2:19 TLB)

The following is one example of how you might use these scriptures to cast this vision. This is simply an example of one way to cast this vision. You can use any or all of this, or do something completely different. What's important is that you cast a vision that will convict your people of the benefit of attending your rally and joining a small group.

Week One

The key in week one is to begin building relationships. Talk about our relationship to God and how it affects our walk with God. It's amazing how many people don't really understand the relational heart of God. Also talk about the importance of our relationships with one another. Use week one to begin to tie our relationship with God to the kind of relationships a small group can create. Show people how small groups can be the key to building the kinds of relationships God wants in our lives.

It's also a good time to discuss the relationships we currently have that are keeping God from being the center of our lives. By the end of week one your people should know how important relationships are and they should begin to see how a small group is the answer to that issue. Introduce the rally, but don't focus on it this week. Week one is only the groundwork leading up to the full push.

Week Two

Week two is designed to take relationships to the next level. Now you begin to explore the difference between the biblical definition of fellowship and the world's definition of fellowship.

Fellowship in the world means hanging out with your buddies, fishing with friends, going to movies together, eating together, and so on. But how does that compare to the biblical meaning of fellowship?

The word "fellowship" comes from the Greek word *koinonia*, which means "putting good deposits into each other." While hanging out with friends or eating a meal together is fellowship, those things don't meet the biblical standard for fellowship. These things fall under the term "socializing." You will be surprised to see how many people don't understand the difference between socializing and fellowshipping.

"Putting good deposits into each other" means sharing your struggles, failures, and successes. It means loving each other through the good and bad of life. It is the kind of relationship that small groups are based on. Here's an example of the difference. Recently, I (John) was at one of our best small groups led by one of my small group coordinators. While talking about what the group has meant to each person, one of the ladies in the group said that she and her husband had been going to the church for five years and had never joined a small group or served in a ministry. The church was a place they spent an hour a week and nothing more. Finally, after all those years they decided to join a small group. In tears, she said, "We reluctantly came to this group because we really didn't know anyone at church. After being in the group for a year I realized I had shared things with this group of strangers that I had not shared with my closest friends."

This is the kind of fellowship God craves for us. They had plenty of friends and social events, but none of them filled the place in their hearts that the small group had filled. She and her husband now regularly attend their group, and she serves faithfully each week as a team leader in the greeting ministry. She talks about how their lives have changed and credits their small group for those changes. If you have any stories past or present of this nature, be sure to include them in your messages.

During this phase, talk about another big misconception—the difference between the worship experience and fellowship. The two are not the same, but most people think they are. Most people think that they are actually taking care of both parts when they go to church on the weekend, when in fact they are two completely separate parts of their walk with God. Worship is vertical; its purpose is to worship God and God alone. Fellowship is more horizontal and is important to support the worship experience and make it more lasting and meaningful.

Be careful to explain that fellowship doesn't replace worship or vice versa. To explain the difference, you can tell people that if worship really was fellowship, the pastor should be able to randomly ask people in the service to come up on the stage, shove a microphone in their face, and ask them to share their deepest fears, hurts, and failures so the congregation can help them. Can you imagine the look on people's faces? What this does is help people understand just how different each of these parts of their walk with God is. It helps them begin to see that God wants people in their lives to help them deal with those kinds of life issues. By the end of this part of the sermon series, the people should begin to understand why they need to be in a small group.

One of the best things you can do throughout this series, if you have video capabilities, is make videos of people in your ministry sharing their stories of how small groups have changed their lives. There is nothing more powerful and convicting than regular people from the church sharing life-change stories. You may not have these testimonies at first because your ministry is new, but you will have them for your second rally if your groups are doing what they are designed to do. If you have the ability to make video testimonies like this, then make sure you do it. Keep the video to no more than five or ten minutes per person. It will take that much raw video to come up with a good minute to a minute and a half of video. It is worth whatever it takes to get it done.

Week Three

Week three is all about small groups and the rally. Now you can begin to share specifically what a small group is, why they are so important, and how their lives will be changed through them. Newer people may not even have a clue what a small group is, so this is the time to explain to people what they can expect. Talk about all the different types of groups that are available, and explain that you have a group for each of them. Along the way you will certainly be using scripture to make each point, but make sure that every point this week ends with, "Come to the small group rally today."

Along the way you will hear just about every excuse you can imagine as to why some people aren't joining small groups. Here are some examples of the reasons you can expect to hear for those who are looking for an excuse not to attend: I'm too old. I'm too young. My life is too messed up. I don't know enough about the Bible. Small groups are not deep enough (that one really irritates me). I'm divorced. There probably isn't a group for me. I'm afraid I won't fit in. I'm afraid to walk into a room full of people.

These are all valid concerns and fears, but the key to getting past them is to address them before they are brought up. Use the series you are teaching to address these issues as you cast the vision for the ministry and the rally.

Make sure during the series you address the following key issues:

- What does God say about small groups?
- Why is small group fellowship key to their growing in their walk with God?
- Why are small groups so important to the future growth and success of the church?
- What is a small group, and what isn't it?
- And, most important, by the end of this series does every person in our church know the day and time of the rally and why they need to come?

To be able to answer those questions you need to first make sure that the small group leadership and the senior pastor agree with what those answers are.

When we do a rally at BAF Pastor Bil always says the same thing at the end of the last week of the sermon series: "If you're not in a small group, I expect to see you today at 5:00 right here in the sanctuary. I'll see you then."

This is only one example of how you can get your church on board with this ministry. It is a guideline to help you understand what the goal of the sermon series is and how to get the focus on the upcoming rally. Use your imagination and your understanding of the people God has called to your church, and create a series that works for you.

Other Methods to Fill Up Small Groups

Every small group should be adding people by personal invitation. Anyone who attends the group can and should be inviting other people to join the group.

Here are some options you can use to make sure that small groups are on the mind of every person who comes to church on an ongoing basis.

- If you have a weekly bulletin that has an information tear-off, add a box that can be checked that says something like, *"I am interested in joining a small group."* Separate those out and send them to someone you have assigned to collate them and pass them on to your small group leaders or your small group coordinators.
- Make up a "Join a Small Group" insert or handout that each person coming to church receives and can fill out. On that insert make sure you say what a small group is and why people need to join one, and have blank lines where they can fill in their contact information. The insert should contain nothing but information about small groups and how to sign up.
- BAF put the inserts in the bulletin at least once or twice per month.
- Set up a small group table in your lobby area. For all services, staff it with experienced small group leaders. Have a handout ready to give to anyone interested. Also make sure you have information cards so you can sign people up on the spot.
- Have a small group page set up on the church Web site. Make sure you have online sign-up capabilities set up as well. When someone goes to the BAF Web site and fills out that form, it is transmitted to my (John's) office. If you don't have that capability then at least make sure there is contact information

available. We don't recommend putting personal information or directions to the homes where the groups meet. We don't think it's safe to put that kind of information out there for any and everyone. We realize that kind of information is readily available, but we don't think you should be able to find it on our church Web site. Also, it is counterproductive to provide a list of all the small groups that are available. It is best to send people to a specific group because it keeps the leaders from getting tons of phone calls only to end up forwarding these people to a better group. It also keeps people from hopping around to one group after another only to find out that those particular groups aren't really for them.

- Do a database mailer. Make up a mailer and send it to everyone you have in your database. Use the same content that you use on the weekend handout. The mailer is a personal invitation to join a small group. Find ways to make the mailer personal because people respond to anything they feel is personal.
- Have this same form with a fill-out section available in your lobby area all the time for anyone who wants it.
- Use your imagination and find what works best for your church.

What if you do all the work and have all the leaders you could ever want trained and ready to go, but you don't have enough people to fill up your small groups? When this happens it usually means that step one and step two weren't really completed and the vision of the leadership wasn't big enough and cast often enough. You or your leadership need a bigger and more passionate vision of what small groups can do, and you need to start over with casting and recasting the vision.

Moving On

We've spent a lot of time talking about how you can fill up your groups once you have them ready to go. All of these things work well, and if you use a combination of them you should have some success. However, all these ideas are simply tools to give people a chance to sign up for a group. What is more important is that you understand that the tools only work because they support a vision. You can use all the tools you want, but without casting and recasting the vision for why people need to join a small group, the tools will have limited success.

The churches that have growing, healthy, life-changing small group ministries are the churches who believe in them enough to make vision-casting a priority. The vision will only stay strong and active if you are willing to do whatever it takes to keep that vision alive in the hearts and minds of the people in your church. Success will not happen by accident; it will only happen if you make it happen.

Coaching Time

- Whatever obstacles you have to doing a small group rally, find solutions to them. The rally will get people to join your groups, so use it.
- Use every idea you come up with to get people to join small groups. When you have used them all up, then go back to some you no longer use and try them again.
- Whatever you do just make sure you're always promoting small groups in some way.

Note

1. Rick Warren, *The Purpose-Driven Life* (Grand Rapids: Zondervan, 2002), 130.

CHAPTER ELEVEN

AFFINITY GROUPS: PART ONE

Step Eleven: Create the Appropriate Small Groups

A small group ministry can be designed in many ways. We know some churches that use the geographical system, which places people in groups based on where they live due to the travel time involved in getting from place to place. If you live in a large metropolitan city that system might work well for you. But in the vast majority of cases we prefer the affinity model—keeping people in groups with other people pretty much in the same station in life.

We've found that couples with babies or young children prefer to be with other couples with kids the same age. In the same way, couples with older kids usually don't want to be with a house full of small babies because they are generally past that time in their lives. Are these examples always true? No, which is why this is a model to follow, not an absolute.

We think you should give leaders a lot of leeway to create a group that fits who they are. However, for the protection of those attending groups, use common sense. As an example, there should never be single men in their thirties to fifties attending groups with young adults in their twenties. If a single man wants to be in that group he is usually there for the wrong reasons. Another example is that you shouldn't allow people who are separated to attend singles groups. You don't want to encourage divorce, and any persons who begin to act single before they are actually single will most likely end up single. But other than a few specific situations like these, allow leaders to determine what they want their group to be.

Because the leader was convinced it would work, I (John) have allowed someone to set up a group that I was sure was doomed from the beginning. I have done this because I believe the process of trying and failing can be a positive tool to a leader's growth. But, more important, as leaders we must also be humble enough to let people try something on the chance they might be right. Give people a chance to succeed, and if they fail use that situation to grow them.

Below is a list for how BAF uses affinity groups. From a leadership standpoint each of these groups is different and brings unique challenges in management.

- Married couples with young kids
- Married couples with older kids
- Young couples with no kids
- Older couples with no kids
- College and young adult singles (18-25)
- Late twenties and early thirties singles
- Late thirties and forties singles
- Fifty and over singles
- Women's Groups
- Men's Groups
- True affinity groups (running, scrapbooking, sports, etc.)
- Groups that are unique and don't follow any model

The idea behind this system is to try to create a group for everyone no matter what their life situation is. It's not realistic to think you will never have that situation where you can't find a fit for someone, but if you create a healthy system you can minimize these instances. If you set up your groups with this type of system, in instances where you don't have a group for someone, it will most likely be a scheduling problem as opposed to a group problem. However, if you find a void that can be filled do so as soon as possible. Unfortunately, at some point you may find that person who just doesn't seem to be able to fit in any group no matter how hard you try. That's usually a personal issue and has more to do with the person than the ministry.

If your ministry is still small you probably won't have a group that fits every situation, but as the ministry grows you will begin to fill the holes as need arises. Don't worry if you don't have all the needs filled when you begin. God will use the unfilled needs to help you determine your next leadership move. In the upcoming chapters we will look at each of these types of small groups and talk about the specific leadership challenges you will face in leading them.

CHAPTER TWELVE

AFFINITY GROUPS: PART TWO

Step Eleven: Create the Appropriate Small Groups

What follows in these two chapters is simply what works at Bay Area Fellowship. It may or may not work in your setting. You have to decide what groups are appropriate. You accomplish this by knowing your congregation and your visitors. So don't copy this model. Instead design groups that meet your needs and grow people into mature people in Christ.

Married Couples

Couples groups are the easiest groups to manage. However, several issues are unique to them.

Childcare

The single biggest issue with married couples groups is childcare. We hear this question all the time—"What do you do about childcare?" Our answer is, do yourself a favor and don't try to come up with an answer. Childcare is the responsibility of each individual group. No other healthy solution exists!

We guarantee you will face this issue if you lead a growing small group ministry. When you begin to get a significant number of groups you will have people come to you with solutions to childcare that involve the church. The best advice we can give you is that small groups happen in homes, not at church. Don't let anyone talk you into having childcare at the church one night a week so all the groups can bring their kids and drop them off. The problems are legion. Everyone who works in childcare has to have background checks and formal training so they know how to deal with emergencies and protect the children. A staff person has to be on site, which means someone has to add another night to an already overworked schedule and your childcare people will be at the church until midnight every night of the week because someone is always going to be late. Also you will have rooms full of exhausted children who just want to go home because it is late. This is not a good option and most of you either already have dealt with it or will in the future.

Don't let anyone talk you into doing your small groups at the church with childcare. You can't create the atmosphere you need for real life-change in small groups around chairs at church. The intimacy and safe feeling of a home cannot be reproduced in the same way at church. That intimacy is so important to creating an atmosphere where strangers will share the deepest hurts of their hearts. Start from day one and make it a part of your leader training: small groups are responsible for their own childcare! Below are some healthy options for childcare.

Childcare Options

- Hire a college or high school student to watch the children in a separate area in the home. Have the group split the cost.
- Hire a college or high school student to watch the children in one of the other homes not being used.
- If there are older kids in the family have them watch the younger kids. (Here's a novel idea: if the kids are old enough to leave at home alone, then leave them at home. It's only a couple of nights a month.)
- Have people use their families to watch the kids a couple of times a month if they are available.
- Just let the kids take care of themselves in your home while you are trying to have the small group experience (this is, by

the way, a horrible option; it will ruin the experience for everyone and will, if it continues, ruin the group).

Counseling Issues

Marital issues come up fairly frequently. If your church is reaching out to the unchurched or new believers of your community, these are also the people who will be coming to your small groups. The unchurched bring with them all the hurts and struggles that come with lives separated from God. These issues will make their way into your small groups.

The most important thing that couples leaders need to know is that while they are to love them through their struggles, they should not become their counselors. There is a big difference between the two, but the line that separates them is not always that clear. When leaders step into the counselor role, and it's easy to do because they want to help, they step into a role they aren't qualified to fill. When that happens you find people who mean well and are really trying to help, but often end up giving bad advice. The best advice for when you see this kind of marital mess is to get the people involved in professional Christian counseling where it can be sorted out by professionals. The group's role is not to be a counselor, it's to be there for support and to love these people through the process.

The Married Couples' System of Management

Most couples want to be with other couples in the same basic age range, because they usually share the same life experiences and often have children in the same age ranges. Kids are really the determining factor here, because couples want to go to groups where their kids can be with other kids around the same age so that they enjoy the experience too. If the kids don't enjoy the experience, it will most likely ruin it for the parents as well. Below is a basic outline of how you can break up these groups.

- Young, newly married couples without kids
- Young couples with kids
- Thirties couples without kids
- Thirties couples with kids

- Forties couples without kids
- Forties couples with kids
- Fifties and sixties couples

And then there are the groups that defy all logic and planning and end up with some kind of crazy mix and love it.

If a group is life-changing, we don't care what you call it or who you invite. Of course, exceptions always exist.

Women's Groups

Women's groups are a tough challenge for any leader. Some women's groups get together to share in issues that women love, and things are great. However, in many cases women's groups are attended by women who have spent their lives making bad choices in men and are now married to ungodly men. Usually these choices were made prior to their relationship with Christ, but they still live with the consequences. These women are emotionally and physically battered, and that creates a tough group to lead. These women are looking for friendship and understanding of their struggles, and they truly want some Christian fellowship to bring some balance to their life and hope for the future. These groups need to be well led, and the women who lead these groups will find the job overwhelming at times.

Many times these groups get going great and are making a difference, but the leaders become emotionally drained. The problem is that a man is usually capable of separating himself from the pain of others, but a woman tends to hurt along with those hurting around her. The struggle with seeing change and growth in these groups is difficult, because the pain is usually coming from a bad spouse, and the only option for healing may seem to be divorce, which the church doesn't want to be seen as endorsing. Just the opposite is true.

Clearly there are situations where the Bible supports divorce, but that is a slippery slope that needs professional counseling, not a lay leader who is trying to find the answers. So what you end up having is a group of women who find themselves stuck in unhealthy relationships. Please hear us here, these groups are great for those attending, because it fills a huge need in these women's lives. But these groups are hard on leaders because women empathize more with those who are hurting, which creates a leader turnover rate that is higher than in other types of groups. So, when needed, allow the leaders to take a break from leadership.

If you are a male who oversees the small group ministry you need to make sure you have a woman who can oversee the women's groups and be there to help leaders before they burn out. Here is a list of some different types of women's groups.

- Deeper Bible Study Home Groups: These are groups of women who want to take on a deeper Bible study in the privacy and intimacy of a home. These groups are usually topical and have a pre-set starting and finishing date.
- Regular Women's Groups.
- Regular Topical Women's Groups: These groups are a combination of the two above. They are groups of women who get together for an extended period of time and are a little more Bible study–driven or geared toward deeper study. Often these groups try to avoid some of the deeper personal struggle issues that other groups focus on. One group tends toward emotional healing, while the other leans toward spiritual growth.

Men's Groups

Not many men want to go to a small group and hang out with a bunch of strangers. The sad part is that almost every Christian man, no matter where he is in his walk, needs to be in one for accountability. Men just don't want to sit down in a group and talk about their fears and pain. It is not a comfortable thing for men to do, especially unchurched men. Just coming to church every weekend is huge in their lives, much less attending a small group full of strangers trying to get them to open up about their lives. By the time they begin to get a grasp of all this, they more often end up in a small group with their wives or other singles. For those who won't go to a men's group try to get them in either a couples group with their wives or a mixed singles group.

The most successful men's groups are usually the ones based on some shared interest like playing softball, hunting, or fishing.

Neither of us called these groups men's groups. Instead, we put them in a category called specialty groups and named them according to their affinity, such as softball. These groups work well because if you can get a man to let down his guard because he is having fun doing what he loves to do, you have a good chance of reaching him through relationships built through the fun of whatever shared interest it is.

If you want your men's groups to be successful you need to talk about real issues that men are dealing with, such as lust, sex, control, arrogance, money, self-righteousness, machismo, and pornography. If you try to make your men's groups some touchy-feely, deep, emotional thing, they won't work. They want someone who is willing to talk to them man to man.

Although you need some men's groups, if we have the choice for a married man to go to a men's group or a couples group with his wife, we always choose the couples group, because that is the single most important relationship in a man's life. Not many men will attend both, so while men's groups are great, get more men in couples groups.

Student Ministry Groups

These groups are done differently than other groups. Junior and senior high school students have some unique issues that you have to deal with for the safety and protection of students as well as the homes where they meet. These groups require a large amount of training and oversight to make sure they are healthy. The best system for training and managing these kinds of small groups can be found at Saddleback Church in California.[1] Pastor Doug Fields and his student ministry team have a system that works well and has all the precautions and training you need to ensure the ministry is healthy.

Celebrate Recovery and Specialty Groups

These groups consist of all the rest of the groups that don't fall under any specific title. Celebrate Recovery groups are small groups that are part of the Celebrate Recovery program, which helps people battle addictions (see http://www.celebraterecovery.com/index.asp). These small groups are real life-change groups, but we don't recommend having them outside of a Celebrate Recovery program. If people in this program are coming to meetings and joining in on small groups, they are placing themselves in a position for God to begin the healing process. But many coming to Celebrate Recovery are not anywhere near healed, and that's why we make sure they are led by trained leaders who understand the disease of addiction.

We also recommend having some specialty groups built around some extra form of affinity other than age or kids. I (Bill) belonged to a small group made up of men who loved to fly their own planes. These groups get together because they enjoy doing the same things and want to make a ministry out of it. Here is a list of some of the specialty groups that John's and Bill's churches had. There is no end to what these can be.

- Cooking Groups
- Scrapbooking Groups
- Running Groups
- Kids' Play Groups
- Single Moms Groups
- Sports Teams Groups
- Motorcycle Groups
- Surfing Groups
- Accountability Groups (all kinds)

The list is endless.

Each group must have the same aspects to it that every other group has. As an example, scrapbooking is fine, but there must be a lesson and prayer too. All groups must be structured for life-change.

Coaching Time

- Childcare issues should be handled by each individual group. No other options will work long term.

- Make childcare options a part of your first leader training. If you do you won't have to deal with it later.

Note

1. You can find this material at http://www.saddlebackfamily.com/home/today.asp.

CHAPTER THIRTEEN

AFFINITY GROUPS: PART THREE

Singles Small Groups

E very small group ministry needs healthy singles groups. The problem is keeping singles groups healthy. We've talked about how things don't just happen, but nothing fits that example more than making sure your singles groups are healthy. They're a tough nut to crack.

At Bay Area Fellowship about 25 percent of the total groups are singles of some type. In that 25 percent is probably 70 percent of the problems experienced in the small group ministry. In Bill's church, 49 percent of the congregation was single, and they populated many of the small groups and caused most of the problems.

While singles groups have their problems, it's important to know that the rewards outweigh the problems. So make sure you have singles groups, but be sure you carefully manage them.

Be Aware of the Issues before You Begin

Before starting singles groups it's important to understand the dynamics of single men and women so you'll understand the

103

unique issues you may face in these groups. The messes you have to clean up in singles groups are usually a lot worse than those in couples groups. Singles will come to your groups with a lot of negative baggage that creates an atmosphere where people, women in particular, can get hurt. This may sound a bit melodramatic, but when you clean up a couple of these messes you will begin to see things in a different light.

The level of temptation singles face today is enormous. Everywhere they turn, society fills them with a dumbed-down version of morality that can never satisfy the soul. Consider the morality promoted every night on prime-time television. Then add the overwhelming effects of Internet pornography, and you have a mess.

Why are some singles so susceptible? If you're lonely and looking for something to fill an emptiness that only God can fill, what could be more alluring than beautiful women or handsome men and a promise of sex, parties, and every kind of fun that pleases the human body. When you take away the regular intimacy married couples have, you have an explosive emotion that can easily be set off in a small group. On top of those temptations, singles are also confronted with the need to fit in. These are powerful pulls on a person that can lead a person down a track he or she wouldn't normally go down, and singles go down that track often.

Having said that, let us also say how important and worthy the effort is. Singles small groups create an opportunity for singles to have a choice between finding a date for the night at a bar during the last round of drinks and developing lasting godly relationships in a small group. Having that choice is critical because many singles don't realize there is a choice.

Finding the Right Men Is Crucial and Difficult

We don't want to pick on men, but if you look at the singles ministries in most churches you'll find more women than men trying to walk with God. Men seem to be more susceptive to temptation than women. Finding God-honoring Christian single men worthy of leading a small group is difficult. The wrong choice in single male leaders can be fatal to your singles ministry. When it comes to choosing single men to lead, you must be extremely careful. You need men you know who are truly men of character and honor.

These choices are so critical because when you reach into a lost world, many of the women you reach come with lives that represent bad choices in men. Many of these women come believing they need a man to give them a sense of significance. These women are vulnerable to a smooth-talking, good-looking man who appears on the outside to be walking with God only to find out it was all an act. One of the hardest things for a Christian single to do is to have the patience needed to wait on God to bring to them the person God has chosen for them. That lack of patience is what can cause women to not see character flaws until it's too late. By that time it's hard to walk away and admit your mistake. Loneliness clouds good judgment, and many men will prey on that weakness.

For the Strong, Confident, Successful, Single Woman

If you're a strong, confident, successful, single woman and take issue with what we are saying, we're proud that you have it all together and that God has blessed you with strength and confidence, so please don't take offense. However, far more single women have a life filled with the consequences of the poor choices they have made. Many are single moms who are truly struggling to get by month to month. More women than not have hearts and spirits that are wounded by the bad men they have allowed into their lives. Many single women are raising their kids alone because the men they chose were poor husbands and fathers. So instead of getting angry with us, join a small group and help these women retake the spirits that were stolen from them. Become a model for the women who want to change their futures and make the kind of choices that will rebuild their spirits.

Why Men Can Be a Problem

Men can be a problem because they are visual animals. There is nothing that arouses a man more quickly than the presence of a beautiful woman. With what has become acceptable in how

105

women dress, it's remarkable that any man gets through the day without spending half of it on his knees asking God to forgive him for the last thought he wishes he hadn't had. The men who come to your groups are exactly like the men in the Bible—completely flawed. In an attempt to help leaders prepare for the struggles of singles small groups, here's a list of the sins single men struggle with.

- Lust
- Money
- Success
- Control
- Pride
- Self-righteousness
- Power
- Arrogance

Please understand that every man has some or all of these, so we're really just talking about the extremes. You won't ever have a group full of men who are horrible at all of the above, but you need to learn to recognize when a man in a group has real issues with any of the above.

Watch and Control the Predators

Watch for predators in your small groups. If you find one, remove him from the ministry before more damage is done! He'll be mad at you and say all kinds of things about you, but removing him is better than knowing you failed to protect another woman in the ministry. Challenge the good men in your groups to watch over the ministry and protect the women in their groups.

We should say that once in a great while the predator is a woman. Although such instances are rare, they are just as devastating.

Please don't let any of this scare you away from having singles groups, because they are awesome and so many people's lives will be changed through them. The reason we have taken so much time to talk about singles and the things they bring to your groups is because the consequences from these behaviors can do so much damage to your ministry and to the people in them. The key to minimizing this damage is to talk openly about what to look for.

If you train your singles small group leaders to recognize this kind of behavior, then you can avoid the pitfalls that come from it.

Confrontation Can Lead to Change

One of the good things that comes from recognizing this kind of behavior is that you have a chance to confront people with their issues. Doing so gives you a chance for real life-change.

On a number of occasions we have had to ask men, and occasionally women, to stop attending small groups due to the damage they were leaving in their paths. But we have also had the chance to see people change the way they live their lives because they were confronted. Some of those people lead small groups now. That's the kind of life change you can expect from your singles small group ministry if you will do what you need to do to keep it healthy.

Don't assume just because your leaders are single that they're prepared to deal with these kinds of issues. The way to prepare leaders is to spend time with them, teach them, and lead them. Find creative ways to talk about these issues. I (John) regularly have singles leaders in my home talking about the tough issues and how to deal with them. I challenge them not to let character issues go unconfronted, to protect the women of the ministry, and to be willing to deal with these kinds of character issues before someone gets hurt. Most important, I challenge the leaders to make sure they are walking with God so they can have some authority when dealing with this stuff.

If you are a small group leader and need help in this area, rely heavily on your singles coordinator. Let that person be your eyes and ears to the issues in this ministry. Your coordinator has been in these groups regularly, has built a solid relationship with each leader, and knows some of the issues in your group.

If you are a small group coordinator, the most important thing you can do to ensure a healthy small group system is to make sure you lead your leaders. Don't just throw them out there and hope for the best. Leaders need to know they have someone they can go to for help.

When leaders come with issues, use that time to lift them up and to thank them for caring enough to come to you. Help them grow and face a problem and deal with it, and help them make a tough decision if necessary, even if it's contrary to their personality. Dealing with issues is the best time to encourage and grow your leaders.

Singles Small Group System

Small group systems come in a variety of styles. We know a number of churches that break their groups up geographically because of the size of the city they are in. Others develop their small groups around affinity. Still others assign people to small groups. Although we will show you how BAF does it, it is important that you figure out a system that fits your church and your personality as a leader.

BAF uses a system based on age and affinity. Corpus Christi is a city of only about 300,000 people, so within the city you can pretty much get to anywhere in the city within twenty minutes. This makes it easy for us to break our groups up by age and common interest (affinity) because the geographic issue is not our main concern. In particular with singles, the age thing is very important for obvious reasons. A good example is if you have a fifty-year-old guy wanting to go to the college or even young twenties groups. Trust us, that's a bad idea.

Even though we primarily place people by ages, we also have some outlying cities with small groups, but we still try, if possible, to follow the same plan. It is so important with singles to make sure you keep people pretty much in the same age range so you don't create unnecessary problems.

Provide some options for separated people such as men's groups, women's groups, or couples groups who welcome singles. We hope you will have some couples groups who welcome people who are separated. People who are separated need to be either with healthy married couples or people of the same sex, not with fun-loving single people. Our hope is that the members of the married group can possibly change the heart of someone committed to divorce.

Here is a list of how BAF breaks up their singles Hometeams.

- **Connect Groups**—Connect groups are the young adults from the college and young professional ministry. These groups are basically eighteen to twenty-eight-year-olds, and they are lead by young adults from that ministry.

- **Twenties Groups**—These are the young adults who are a little older than the connect group, but still in their late twenties or early thirties. We have these groups both with and without kids. This is one of the places where a lot of young, single moms go.
- **Mid Thirties and Early Forties Groups**—This group is usually for the single parents and people who are in a different place in life based on life experience. You can mix this group up pretty safely because the maturity level is usually there. Many are single parents, and we have these groups both with and without kids.
- **Forties Groups.**
- **The Nameless Group**—This group is tough to name because no matter what name you give them it will be wrong.

However you design your singles small group system, make sure it's as inclusive as possible and be prepared to have those groups that just don't fit any model.

We Love Singles

We don't want you to feel like this chapter is a negative look at the life of singles, because it isn't. We do, however, want you to lead with your eyes open to the potential problems you may face, and if you're a growing church and your groups are multiplying, you will deal with some of the issues we've mentioned. We just want you to be prepared.

So, hear our heart: we love singles and want them to have a life-changing experience in your small groups. When you choose strong single leaders, train them, support them, lift them up, and believe in them, you create an awesome tool for life-change and your church will be stronger because of it.

Coaching Time

- Make sure that you both love singles as well as have a healthy respect for the problems they can cause.

- Don't go out of your way looking for problems, but familiarize yourself with what can happen so you are prepared when it does. Notice we didn't say "if."
- Have you honestly accepted the fact that you are going to have some problems in your singles groups?
- Are you prepared to deal with these problems, and have you prepared your leaders to deal with them? Spend extra time training and retraining your singles small group leaders. It is worth the extra effort to avoid some of the problems that will occur.

CHAPTER FOURTEEN

THE END OF THE BEGINNING

Well, now you have all of the information you need to either grow your present small groups or to begin a new small group system. What are you waiting for? Isn't it time to get your church connected, so that it can be a safe place where people can grow in their faith?

Let's review the steps one more time just to make sure that you have them under your belt.

Step One: Bring the Lead Pastor on Board

No one has the ability to promote small groups like the pastor. Without your pastor on board, the system is doomed from the beginning.

Step Two: Convince the Powers That Be

Building a small group system is hard enough when you have the structure of the church behind you. Without the power structure behind you, your efforts will be less than effective.

Step Three: Build a Small Group Management System

The worst thing that can happen is for you to begin your small group system without a plan for how to handle its growth. What if it explodes and you are the only one trained to lead it?

Step Four: Pray for and Create a Culture of Multiplication

The number one mistake leaders make in starting small groups is that they do not embed multiplication in the DNA from the beginning. If you want your small group system to be the most effective system you can design, then make sure every leader understands that multiplication of the small group within the first year is one of the primary goals.

Step Five: Find Effective Small Group Leaders

It is better to go slow and find effective leaders, than to start big with leaders who either aren't trained or don't have the passion for small groups.

Step Six: Develop Several Levels of Leadership

Don't be afraid to empower and delegate authority to your best leaders. Doing so will allow your small groups to outgrow your ability to handle them. Keep in mind that at the heart of any effective small group ministry is leadership development.

Step Seven: Avoid Problem People

Over time you will learn to avoid certain people. In the beginning you will probably make some mistakes. Learn from them and go on, but weed out problem people from leadership. Don't be afraid to exercise Matthew 18.

Step Eight: Train Your Leadership

In busy times like today you will have to figure out the best way to train your leadership. We feel that on-the-job training through the coordinators, sprinkled with monthly and annual training, is the best way. However you decide to do your training, just make sure you do it. Casting a vision for multiplication in your small groups begins at the new leader's very first training. For a vision to stay alive it must be recast over and over at every training event.

Step Nine: Create Ownership

The role of the small group leader is to create a safe place where people feel like they belong. The key to creating a healthy small group is for everyone attending to take ownership of the group. Ownership will only happen when every person has an active role in the group. When everyone has an active role in the group then they will begin to call the group "my group" instead of "the group." That's when real life-change begins.

Step Ten: Fill Your Small Groups

Small groups don't just fill up on their own. You must design ways for people to regularly enter your groups, and you need a system for getting people from the pew to the small group and keeping them there.

Step Eleven: Create the Appropriate Small Groups

We've never seen two effective small group systems that look identical when it comes to the type and number of small groups. Don't be afraid to have a system of groups in place, but also be flexible to the Spirit in allowing unexpected groups to emerge.

Two more last reminders: Appreciate, encourage, and support your leaders any chance you get. The majority of your small group ministry will be led by volunteers. Volunteers need to know the leadership appreciates their commitment and that someone truly cares about their particular group. Appreciation can be shown in many ways. Use them all, but none are more powerful than personal words of encouragement.

And finally, pray for God to bless your efforts. As the ministry leader you need to pray. Pray for the small groups ministry; pray for current and future small group leaders; pray for the people attending small groups; pray for your church; and because you have been called to cast the vision and grow the ministry, pray for your own leadership. The most important key to every growing and healthy small group ministry is God. Don't ever forget this.

Now go and work your small group ministry.

HOMETEAM COORDINATOR COVENANT

The following covenant is used at Bay Area Fellowship. We offer it here as a model for one you might use with your own congregation.

I. Commitment

A. I will commit 4-6 hours per week on Hometeam-related issues. In this time I will do the following:
1. Visit each Hometeam two to three times per year.
2. Have Hometeam leaders in my home two times per year for relationship-building and ongoing training (budget money available).
3. Promptly distribute names to available Hometeams and make sure that those that were not placed in a group are refunded in a timely manner.
4. Have regular communication with the Hometeam director and pastor.
5. Ensure that each Hometeam and leaders have the current BAF curriculum.
6. Commit to pray for the Hometeam leaders that God has entrusted with us.
B. I will instill leadership characteristics in the leaders in my group.
C. I will commit to maintaining Hometeam leader motivation.

II. Communication

A. I will maintain regular communication with the BAF Hometeams director and pastor (e-mail, phone, conversations, etc.).
B. I will maintain regular two-way communications will all Hometeam leaders.
C. I will be dedicated to building meaningful personal relationships with every leader in my group.

III. Accountability

A. I will attend monthly coordinator meetings and be prepared to give a reasonable account of the status of my groups.
B. I will hold myself accountable to the BAF leadership for how I represent the church at all times.
C. I am a member of Bay Area Fellowship and am committed to a biblical tithe in support of the BAF mission.

Hometeam Coordinator Covenant Statement

1. I agree and will comply with the BAF Hometeam Coordinator Covenant.
2. I am committed to the vision and leadership of Bay Area Fellowship.
3. I understand that the failure to comply with the Coordinator Covenant can result in dismissal.
4. I understand as a Hometeam coordinator that I am a part-time employee of BAF. (This is something that happened when we got to 150 groups. This will come later as the ministry grows.)

Signature: _____ Date: _____

Hometeam Leader/Host Covenant

As a Hometeam Leader/Host, I will commit to the following:

1. I will commit to completing Class 101, signing the covenant, and backing it.
2. I will commit to completing Class 201 and following the steps it lays out.
3. I will support and defend the vision and direction of Bay Area Fellowship and its leadership.
4. I will recognize that as a Hometeam leader I represent Bay Area Fellowship at all times.
5. I will commit to actively multiplying my group by seeking and training potential new leaders from within my group. I will commit to that multiplication a minimum of one time per year.
6. I will commit to regular weekend service attendance.
7. I will commit to faithfully attend ongoing training or appreciation events.
8. I will maintain regular communication with my coordinator and ministry leadership.
9. I understand that the failure to comply with the Leader/Host Covenant can result in dismissal.

As a Hometeam leader at Bay Area Fellowship I will commit to the above covenant.

Signature: _____   Date:_____

Spouse's Signature: _____ Date: _____

APPENDIX B

CURRICULUM

The problem with most materials for small groups is that they are primarily designed for Bible studies, and you know how we feel about that. The problem with the Bible studies that are adaptable to small groups is that most are ten to twelve weeks long; and by the time a small group has been in a study for six weeks, they're already bored with it because it's just too long and too in-depth, and to do it right homework is required. Asking small groups to read and do homework during the week will end up killing the group. Small groups must be relationally driven, and Bible studies aren't created for that forum. There's nothing wrong with Bible studies; they just need to be used in the proper forum.

An even bigger problem you will run into is that if you have a twelve-week study in a small group that meets twice a month, then you add the fun days when groups just get together to eat and fellowship, then a meeting that gets canceled for some reason, you then have one very expensive study in only one small group for six months or longer. So let's look at some options and talk about the highs and lows of each.

The Weekend Message

The weekend message is a good option, especially for new or smaller small group ministries. In the beginning of our ministry at

Bay Area Fellowship I (John) and another pastor would take turns taking the weekend message and turning it into curriculum for small groups. This is a great option, but be sure when preparing the material for small groups that you make it shorter than the message and designed to create discussion. No one wants to hear the message preached again. This is a great option as long as someone has the time to write the curriculum.

The second issue when using the weekend message is distribution. People are busy and many leaders either do not take the time to pick up the material, or they are not as prepared to teach as they needed to be, or they get it late or don't have a chance to look at it. However, with the advances made in e-mail, you may find using the weekend message to be highly advantageous in helping people feel connected.

Sermons

The second thing we tried was to purchase sermons on family topics so that we had some VCR curriculum available for those whose lives were busy. This method was very good and worked well for a long time and was very reasonably priced. The downside is that not everyone is drawn to that kind of curriculum, so it wasn't a complete fix. It was hard to find sermons that were topical and weren't so long that groups got bored. This is a reasonable option if you do your homework and pick sermons that are topical and life-applicable.

Books

Books are great and work well in a small group. You can find them on every topic and have an endless stream of curriculum. One downside is that you have to have a very strong leader to teach out of a book. The leader has to be willing to prepare at a much higher level and write his or her own discussion questions. You will have leaders in your ministry who can do this, and who actually love to do this. We still have groups at BAF that use books. But these exceptionally strong leaders are few and far between. Another downside is that while books can make great small group curriculum, in the hands of the wrong leader they are boring and turn into a leader doing nothing but talking and teaching. Books are not the long-term fix for small group curriculum.

DVDs

In the last few years we have begun to see some really good curriculum being produced specifically for small groups. The relational style of small groups is taking off in this country because churches are seeing real life-change happening in them. We believe these curricula are so good that they are the future of small group curriculum. This type of curriculum opens up a world of potential leaders who have the gift of hospitality but don't feel like they are qualified to teach. With this kind of curriculum the teaching is biblical and sound, and all the leader has to do is make people feel welcome and create a discussion about what has already been taught. Here are some options we've found to be exceptional.

Doing Life Together Series

Life Together is a company run by Brett Eastman. Brett has served on the small group staff at both Saddleback and Willow Creek and is now creating some great small group curricula. The material is designed to be a twenty-minute teaching on a life-applicable topic with study guides that have discussion questions. The Doing Life Together series is a six-DVD series with six weeks of curriculum on each DVD. You can purchase this curriculum at www.lifetogether.com.

The Purpose-Driven Life

Another great DVD curriculum is Rick Warren teaching his book *The Purpose-Driven Life*. The book, of course, is one of the best sellers ever, but with the DVD curriculum you actually have Pastor Rick teaching you each chapter. He does about a twenty-minute overview of each chapter, then you have leader's guides so you can discuss the application of these issues to your everyday life. This is a great curriculum idea and is again designed specifically for small groups. Almost every small group at Bay Area Fellowship has gone through this curriculum.

Willow Creek Association Curriculum

For those who just don't like to use a DVD curriculum, you can go to www.willowcreek.com, then go to Resources, and then Bible Studies. There you will find written small group curricula on every subject you can possibly imagine. Don't let the Bible Studies link deter you; these books are created for small groups and are some of the best written curricula available.

Another excellent source for curriculum is SmallGroups.com. They provide resources from launching a small group to training the coaches and directing the entire ministry.

These examples are very good, and the number of choices continually grows. However, be careful when choosing material because much of it leans toward deep biblical teaching, and that type of teaching just doesn't work well in the small group model.